planted

A GUIDED STUDY TO PRODUCE A PEACE-FILLED LIFE IN AN ANXIETY-FILLED WORLD

COLETTE SCHAFFER

WESTBOW
PRESS®
A DIVISION OF THOMAS NELSON
& ZONDERVAN

WestBow Press books may be ordered through booksellers or by contacting:

WestBow Press
A Division of Thomas Nelson & Zondervan
1663 Liberty Drive
Bloomington, IN 47403
www.westbowpress.com
1 (866) 928-1240

ISBN: 978-1-9736-8444-2 (sc)
ISBN: 978-1-9736-8445-9 (hc)
ISBN: 978-1-9736-8443-5 (e)

Library of Congress Control Number: 2020901416

Print information available on the last page.

WestBow Press rev. date: 02/20/2020

dedication

To Jesus Christ:
My everything, the One I am planted in.

To my husband, Bryce:
You are the love of my life
and the encourager of my dreams.
Thank you for your love and support
as you have helped me to fulfill God's plan for my life.

To my children:
Ethan, Callie, and Nathanial,
my cheerleaders and much inspiration.
You are great examples of living a life planted in Christ.

Acknowledgment

I would like to acknowledge and thank my dear friends Bobbi Maher and Robi Miller for their assistance in editing the first draft of this book.

I would also like to thank all of the ladies who took time to participate in the book study for my recordings – you are greatly appreciated.

Most of all, I would like to thank those who have been lifting me and this project up in prayer. I love you all!

Contents

Introduction

As I have scrolled through my Facebook feed and listened to those around me, I hear and see a theme that has plagued so many people. That theme is anxiety. Whether the cause is from the busyness of life or stems from a fear of something, the symptoms of anxiety are sly and misleading. It really wasn't until I read an article about what high-functioning anxiety looks like that I was able to recognize exactly what had been plaguing me for so many years. I was equally shocked to realize just how prevalent the anxiety issue was and is.

The sad thing is that the symptoms of anxiety are so misleading that although I sought out medical help for some of my symptoms, the doctors I went to couldn't or didn't catch on to the root of my problems. I had even told one doctor that I thought my symptoms might be from stress, but the doctor seemed to dismiss the notion since my outward persona was calm and in control.

Part of my healing process was realizing that I wasn't alone – that the symptoms I faced day in and day out were not just in my head. I am positive that if I could have been able to identify the cause of the bizarre, seemingly irrational symptoms that haunted me daily, I would have healed much quicker. The good news is that I am now free from those frequent panic attacks. Anxiety still tries to give me fits now and then, but I have learned how to use it to recognize the root of the issue and deal with it quickly. It is no longer in control of me.

I hadn't really thought about sharing my story about living with anxiety and how I have learned to deal with it until I felt God prompting me to share it with others. I didn't feel like I had much to offer on the subject – I am not an expert by any means. In fact, as a pastor, it was a little tough to open up and examine this subject in my life for all to see, but I knew this was what I was supposed to do. Therefore, I hosted a "Break Free" night at our church and was overwhelmed and surprised by the interest and turnout for the event. Women came with their Bibles and notebooks ready for answers on how to break free from worry, stress, and anxiety.

In the days and weeks that followed the event, I heard testimony after testimony from those in attendance of how the evening had helped them. I was also frequently asked if I was going to host another event like it. I was a little taken back by the response I received and prayed about what God wanted me to do next. As I prayed, the prompting of this book kept coming to me. So, it is again out of obedience to God that I am writing and sharing with you what I have learned.

It is my prayer that as you read this book, you will find practical and spiritual insight that can be applied to your unique situation. This book can be used in a group Bible study setting or individually. I encourage you to:

- Highlight and underline portions of the book that speak to you as well as look up the scriptures in your own Bible and take time to think on them.
- Find a journal or notebook to designate as your study notebook and answer the questions and journal prompts at the end of each chapter to get more insight and really engage in the process of living a peaceful life.
- Take advantage of the more in-depth teaching for each chapter from the QR code provided with the journal prompts. Simply scan the code with your smartphone camera or download a QR code reader app. You can also access the videos on my website at schafferministries.com. (QR Code is registered trademark of DENSO WAVE INCORPORATED.)

As you begin to put these biblical principles into practice, you will experience more peace in your life than ever before. I pray that you may understand just how much God loves you and how He created you to operate in this life. Most importantly, I pray that you learn how to maintain that freedom and live in a place of peace all the time. That's right! I said ALL THE TIME. Trust me, it is possible! Are you ready to have your life transformed?

Let's start!

chapter one

I'VE BEEN THERE |

I did it. I became (according to the Anxiety and Depression Association of America) one of the 40 million people in America who suffers or has suffered from some sort of anxiety. I personally think the amount is far greater since there are many individuals, like myself, who have or had undiagnosed anxiety.

We all have a picture in our minds of how we should or would like to be – at least I always did. Two of my favorite characters growing up were Wonder Woman and Mary Poppins - funny combination I know. If it was possible, I was going to be the perfect combination of those characters. Wonder Woman was beautiful and powerful. She wasn't afraid of anything and, best of all, had an invisible jet! I mean, who wouldn't want an invisible jet, right? Mary Poppins was, of course, "Practically Perfect in Every Way." She also had a great British accent and had an amazing cleaning technique!

So, I found myself trying my best to be the perfect combination of Wonder Woman and Mary Poppins – "Wonder Poppins" if you will! I have always been a positive person, a mentally strong person, and a healthy person. I was raised in a Christian home and have heard my Savior's voice my whole life. I have an amazing husband and three exceptional children. I say all of this not to brag about my life - but to say that depression, anxiety, and stress do not discriminate. I didn't know that my heart racing unexplainably was a sign of anxiety and stress revealing itself. The thought never occurred to me because I was the one who was supposed to have it together, the one that other people came to for help as a pastor and a friend.

THE BEGINNING

I went to the doctor with some of my symptoms, such as my heart pounding irregularly. In fact, I was fitted with a heart monitor to track the irregularities that I complained about, but never found anything abnormal. According to the doctor, I was fine. So, I reasoned my symptoms away and kept living the life that was slowly killing me.

The symptoms of stress and depression first started after the birth of my youngest son, Nathanial. I had a 4-year old (Ethan), 2-year old (Callie) and now a baby. My family was complete, and I was living the life I had always dreamt of. I found myself thinking, "If this is what I've always wanted, why don't I feel happy?" Instead of enjoying my life, I felt stressed and sort of numb as I tried to be the perfect mom and wife. "I couldn't be depressed," I told myself, "postpartum depression was something that other women dealt with, not me." I reasoned with myself that I was just tired, that the dark thoughts that would often invade my mind were nothing to be too alarmed with.

A year later, my husband and I answered the call on our lives to be pastors. To do that, we needed first to get our pastoral degrees. So, we decided to move to Tulsa, Oklahoma to attend Rhema Bible Training College. Of course, in true "Wonder Poppins" fashion, as I was packing our little apartment and getting last-minute details done, I was also planning and coordinating my 10th class reunion. STRESSFUL. A week after the reunion, my parents helped drive me, the kids, and our moving truck to Tulsa, Oklahoma to a house we had never seen in person. STRESSFUL. My husband Bryce, stayed back to work a little while longer since he didn't have a job waiting for him. STRESSFUL. So, away I went, very excited (and stressed) to embark on this new chapter of our lives but with no clue what I was in for - Colette, meet the next level of stress and anxiety!

There were many things that contributed to having stress and anxiety with just moving to Tulsa from a small town in South Dakota. The traffic itself gave me anxiety. In addition to the stress of moving, I was going to school and studying, parenting three little ones, and teaching up to 56 private music students at the same time. I know – crazy!!

MAKING ROOM FOR STRESS

Soon I was getting familiar and used to the stress and anxiety that plagued me on a daily basis. It was the way life was, so I accepted it and gave it a place in my life. I remind you that on the outside I had it all together – I was doing what our circumstances and life demanded of me at the time. I also knew that I just had to endure this crazy schedule and life for a short couple of years until we graduated and moved on with our lives in the ministry.

After graduating with our pastoral degrees, we began immediately pastoring a small church in Oklahoma. It was nice to get back to small-town living. As for the stress, I thought it had lightened, but "Wonder Poppins" couldn't be still for too long. The house we had purchased needed constant renovations and our finances were very bleak. Again, I found myself consumed with the "Perfect Syndrome" - being the perfect pastor's wife, perfect mom, and keeping a perfect house. Additionally, I taught around 36 private students, was a substitute teacher, and because I didn't have enough to do – went back to school to finish my Bachelor's degree in Music Education, taking around 18-20 credits each semester.

By the way, there is no such thing as perfect. It is a mirage that will keep evading you at each supposed arrival point. I cared too much about what others thought of me and didn't want to disappoint their perceived idea of who I was. I was often told, "You're so talented and creative! You can do it all!" Truthfully, I liked being recognized as talented and creative, so I did it all. I threw the perfect birthday parties for my kids (before Pinterest). I wrote Sunday school curriculum, including the songs, I wrote VBS curriculum, and the list goes on and on. Looking back, I can see how ridiculous all of that work was. No one can please everyone, and certainly, no one can be perfect– it's not going to happen!

> There is no such thing as perfect. It is a mirage that will keep evading you at each supposed arrival point.

So much of our stress we put on ourselves due to what we believe other people think about us! Why do we care so much? Don't get me wrong; we should care to some extent how those around us perceive us. However, we shouldn't let what others think take priority of what you think about yourself and even greater what God thinks of you.

Honestly, over-extending myself is still an area in my life that I struggle with. However, I am starting to learn that just because I can do something doesn't mean that I am supposed to do it or need to do it. I have also learned to check-in with God before I say yes to add something else to my plate.

The stress I experienced from outside sources such as jobs, school, family, house, church, etc. is one thing, but I also was dealing with issues in my thought life. You see, pastors and ministers are just people like you. We are just as or even more susceptible to attacks from the enemy as anyone else is. I admit that I fell for some of the devil's lies and let him run amuck with my mind. I would dwell on thoughts that I knew were toxic. I didn't fight those thoughts even when I knew I should – besides they were just thoughts, right? How harmful can thoughts be? The answer is *very harmful!* I will discuss later in this book why that was such a huge mistake and how I stopped the torment that I so easily gave way to.

PANIC ATTACKS

The stress that I was under soon turned to what I now know were panic attacks. My heart would feel like it was beating out of my chest. I would work hard to gain control of my breathing with long deep breaths; yet, my chest would still feel as though I had an elephant sitting on it and my throat would feel as though I was being choked. "What was going on with me? Do I need to go to the hospital? Is this a heart attack? Am I going to pass out?" This discussion with myself was a common one. I always came to the same conclusion: "No, Colette, you are fine. Just pray and think about other things. The doctor isn't going to find anything anyway."

I would search for ways to find relief from these 'episodes' and find peace. I would run in place or do jumping jacks really fast to give my heart a reason to beat so hard. I wanted so badly to find relief. The anxiety would come out in other ways as well. I found myself constantly running my fingers through my hair or rubbing my earlobes or earrings. I was irritable, and it didn't take much for me to snap at my kids for little things. Why was I feeling so out of control?

It was while sitting in one of my college classes – a small classroom with peers that I knew fairly well in my field of music education when I started feeling…off. This was a different feeling than I had ever experienced before. I had never quite had *this* sensation of light-headedness mixed with nausea. I couldn't focus on anything around me and had a hard time keeping my head off my desk. That's when I decided I better go find a place to lay down… and here lies the moment I will never forget. I got up to leave, took a few steps, and collapsed on the floor, unable to move, my body totally numb. I could still hear everything going on around me; however, I couldn't summons my body to move. I know I gave my professor and peers a scare that day as they tried to figure out what had happened. I remember thinking, "I'm here. I can understand you. I just can't make myself respond."

I was taken to the urgent care soon after collapsing. They checked my vitals and ran a couple of tests on me to find…nothing! Nothing at all wrong! Unfortunately, they couldn't detect what was really going on. It never crossed their minds that my body just shut itself down from the ongoing stress and anxiety plaguing it.

As I said in the Intro, we all have dealt with stress to varying degrees. There are some healthy types of stress, such as when you are focusing on a task to be completed. This is a short-term stress for achieving goals. However, what I am talking about is not healthy stress at all. This type of stress turns into debilitating anxiety. It finds you like a stray dog and comes home with you whether you like it or not. Some people have learned how to keep the "stray dog" from making a home with them. Others welcome that stinky mess with open arms then wonder why everything else in their house now stinks! I was one of those who saw that "stray dog," thought to myself, "it's harmless enough," and invited that stinky mess home with me.

I know that every person is different and every situation is different, but if you can relate to any of my story please know that there is an answer and a way out! I no longer suffer from panic attacks, and the anxiety that tries to come is easily dealt with. To do this, however, I have had to make changes in my life spiritually, physically, and mentally. Those changes have given me the keys to break free from the bonds of panic attacks and anxiety.

There is freedom for your soul if you will take what I teach in the following chapters and apply it to your life. Change is difficult and hard but not impossible. You might read things in the following chapters that you have never heard before. The things I teach may challenge your current beliefs about God and His Word. However, when I answered the call to the ministry, I took it seriously. I have spent years diligently studying the Bible and developing my relationship with God, both for myself and for others. My "job" is to teach you how to make the Bible real and applicable in your life and situation.

I believe that you are reading this book for a reason. God wants you to live in peace. If you are open to receiving these "truth seeds" in your life, I know they will slowly uproot the anxiety and take over as a root of peace. Ultimately, it will cause the change you so desperately are seeking. You don't have to put up with anxiety and panic attacks anymore!

Take time to consider each reflection question. Ask God to speak to your heart and to reveal things about yourself that you may have never considered. It takes courage to face anxiety head-on. It takes courage to uproot the causes for the anxiety. It takes courage to make the needed changes in your life that will facilitate your victory. Just remember that you are not on this journey alone. God is by your side, and I am cheering you on!

Joshua 1:9 declares, *"Be strong and of good courage; do not be afraid, nor be dismayed, for the Lord your God is with you wherever you go."*

CHAPTER 1

REFLECTION QUESTIONS

1. What are your expectations for yourself? Take a moment to write down everything you are trying to accomplish and be in your life. Are any of these items unrealistic or causing a root of your anxiety?

2. What situations or things have been triggers to activate anxiety in your life?

3. Are there negative things you think about yourself that you know are false, but you buy into them anyway?

4. What physical symptoms have you experienced due to stress or anxiety?

5. Do you view the stress and anxiety that you have dealt with as something you will always deal with, or do you feel hopeful that you can break free from it?

chapter two

WHO ARE YOU? |

There is a scene in *Alice in Wonderland* when the caterpillar is asking Alice who she is. She doesn't know how to answer him – she's not sure who she is. Most people are the same way. They don't truly know who they are or what their purpose in life is. You may totally identify with that. Maybe you have been or felt rejected and have somewhat believed the lies that you are a mistake. If that is you, I want you to listen to me very carefully and re-read what I am about to say. Your circumstances, your upbringing, your social media pages, the color of your skin or size of your clothes, or even what others say about you is NOT who you are. I want you to peel off the hurtful labels that have been stuck to you for too long and open up to the One who knows you best. Knowing God and understanding how He created you is the first step to growing in peace.

> Knowing how God created us is the first step to growing in peace.

YOUR IDENTITY

Many people find their identity in what they are good at. Maybe you were or still are an athlete, a musician, an artist, a singer, or a star student, and you have gotten praise for what you do best. Compliments and praise for what we do – for our talents and abilities feel great; however, if you look to those things for your identity, you will be lost when those talents or abilities are no longer a part of who you are. For example, I have known athletes who identified with being an athlete, but when that season of their life was over, they weren't sure what to do with themselves.

Another dangerous thing to do is to try to find your identity in another person – especially a love interest. I have seen girls bounce from one boyfriend to the next, but the relationships never last. Why? Because they were looking for their own identity in someone else, which will never work. Some find their identities in their roles as a spouse, parent, friend, or a successful businessperson. All of those things are wonderful, but they should be what you do, not who you are.

My husband and I have taught our three children how to drive and have survived to tell about it! When each of our children got behind the wheel for the first time, there were MANY mistakes made. Many "STOPs!" and "SLOW DOWNs," "TURNING SIGNALS ARE GOOD HERE!" Was there anything wrong with our vehicles as soon as our kids got behind the wheel? Of course not - the vehicle was not the problem. The problem obviously was with the knowledge of the one driving. The same is true in your life. You may feel like something is desperately wrong with you because everything you do doesn't seem to work out. However, you may have never read your owner's manual (the Bible) from the perspective of finding out who you really are and what you were created to do. I believe that as you find yourself in the Bible and learn to apply the scriptures to your real-life situations, you will be able to navigate your life in such a way that you will be healthy - spirit, soul, and body. You will find success not defeat.

MADE IN HIS IMAGE

The most important way to really explore who you are and who you were created to be is to learn about how God made you. You are not just a happenstance; the Bible says that you were fearfully and wonderfully made (Psalm 139:14). You were not an accident or an afterthought, but you were knit together with unique qualities and gifts. God loves you so much and has a purpose for you on this earth.

You need first to understand that you are made in the image of God. Genesis 1:26 reads, "*Let US make **man** in OUR image, according to OUR likeness*" *(NKJV emphasis mine)*. Let me point out here that when God said,

"Let Us make *man*," *man* is referring to the human race – both male and female. The beginning of that verse reads, "Let Us." God was referring here to the trinity, God the Father (Himself), God the Son (Jesus), and God the Holy Spirit. Just as there are three persons of the Godhead, humans have three parts as well.

1. Spirit

> Your spirituality is not just a part of you but is the real you.

First and most importantly, you are a spirit being. Almost every religion recognizes the fact that we have a spiritual side. However, you need to realize and recognize that your spirituality is not just a *part* of you but *IS* you. You are a spirit. God designed us to live forever with Him; He never intended death to be a part of our life experience. It wasn't until sin entered the world through Adam and Eve's disobedience that God's intended plan for the human race was changed forever.

2. Body

Next, you live in a body. If you have ever been to a funeral and have seen the body lying in the casket, it is very evident that he or she is not there. The body was just that person's "earth suit." Just as an astronaut needs a spacesuit to withstand the atmosphere of space, we need our earth suit to move around in the earth's atmosphere. This is also the part of us that we tend to default to – meaning that we rely a lot on our surroundings and outside sources to make daily decisions. This isn't all bad – we need our five physical senses to navigate in our world. The problem is that as a Christian, we are not to live solely on those senses – from the outside in but learn to live from the inside out.

> Find out what God created you for and become the very best of whatever that is.

Much of anxiety can stem from our bodies; how we feel about our outward appearance. We are often guilty of letting our bodies dictate to us our worth. It is time that you stop the negative talk about yourself – especially if it is something that can't be changed. Refuse to say another negative thing about your body or about the talents you have or don't have. Comparison to other people and/or negative self-talk is a big source of anxiety. I am very pleased to now see clothing advertisements use models of every shape and size. You are you; Don't spend your time wishing you had someone else's talents or looks or personality. And for goodness sake, don't buy into the lie that if you do 'x amount' of squats, you'll have legs that look like Carrie Underwood's legs. Yes, exercise is good, but your results are going to be the best version of you, not someone else. You have a unique purpose for your talents and personality as well. Find out what God created you for and become the very best at that there is.

3. Soul

The third part of us is our soul. Often the soul gets mixed up with the spirit, but the two are separate. Your soul is your mind, your will, and your emotions. It contains your personality, your likes, and dislikes. The soul is unique in that it is closely related to both the spirit and the body. For example, when you leave this earth, you will still have your personality intact and will be able to recognize your family and friends. In the same regard, science has shown us that memories and our personality reside in our brains. This is why the soul is so misunderstood. Stress, anxiety, and other mental ailments stem from this part of your being as well. Some mental ailments are physical, meaning that they are chemically related and can be altered with a change of diet or medication. However, much of anxiety comes from the spirit/soul relationship. Medications may put a band-aide on the latter to some extent, but the root of those anxieties goes much deeper. We will delve into this topic more extensively throughout this book.

A COPY OF A COPY

As I said, we were created in the image of God. God wanted intelligent beings that would have a personality and the capacity to have a relationship with Him. He wanted beings that would love as He loved, talk as He talked and relate as He related. So, He made a copy of Himself. That original copy had a name – Adam. Then He said to Himself that He could do better and created Eve. JUST KIDDING, guys!

As you know, when you make a copy on a copy machine using an original copy, the image is very close to the original. However, have you ever made a copy from a well-used copy? I am a part-time schoolteacher, so I make a lot of copies for my students. There are times when I will make a copy of a copy because I can't find the original paper - and what is the result? Whatever flaw or mark that was on the copy is now on the rest of the copies. This is what happened when Adam and Eve sinned. They marred the original copy with sin, so now, when a copy is made through reproduction, every copy, no matter how fresh and cute, has the same mark as the original copy – sin. Thank the Lord on High that isn't the end of the story! No, God had a plan to return humans to their original state, and that plan was and is Jesus.

John 3:16 reads, *"For God so greatly loved and dearly prized the world that He even gave up His only begotten Son, so that whoever believes in (trusts in, clings to, relies on) Him shall not perish (come to destruction, be lost) but have eternal (everlasting) life. For God did not send the Son into the world in order to judge (to reject, to condemn, to pass sentence on) the world, but that the world might find salvation and be made safe and sound through Him"* (AMPC).

There is no condemnation in Christ. Everyone is in the same boat, so-to-speak, when they come to Jesus – a flawed copy. It is only through Jesus that you are cleansed and made new. It is only through Jesus that you can find true peace for your soul. It is only through Jesus that you can have real victory over anxiety in your life.

If you have never asked Jesus into your life, now is a good time to do it. Just pray this simple prayer, *"Jesus, I see that I need you in my life. I ask you to come into my heart and forgive me of my sins. I make you the Lord of my life today. Amen."*

A NEW YOU IN A NEW PLACE

Praise God! If you prayed that prayer for the first time or even rededicated your life to Him; the real you, your spirit was recreated! 2 Cor. 5:17 reads, *"Therefore if any person is [engrafted] in Christ the Messiah he is a NEW CREATION – a new creature altogether; the old [previous moral and spiritual condition] has passed away. Behold, the fresh and new has come"* (AMPC).

This means that the real you, your spirit, although still bound to the earth realm and bound to your body, has been transferred into the Kingdom of God (Colossians 1:13-14). Being a citizen of the Kingdom of God has benefits for you to take advantage of, just like being a citizen of the United States. Psalm 103:2-3 says, *"Bless the Lord, O my soul, and forget not all His benefits. Who forgives all your iniquities, who heals all your diseases, who redeems your life from destruction, who crowns you with lovingkindness and tender mercies, who satisfies your mouth with good things, so that your youth is renewed like the eagle's?"* That list of benefits is awesome: forgiveness, healing, love, mercy, and the transforming power of the Word of God. You may not understand all of these things, but they are for you, nonetheless.

To get a better understanding of this concept, picture yourself working in a dead-end job, minimal income, and hardly any benefits to speak of. Then one day, you get transferred out of that job into your dream job. All of a sudden, you have provision and benefits that cover everything you may ever need. Now, say you have been working in your new position for a while but don't know how to access your new benefits. You proceed to handle your life like nothing ever changed - using your minimal benefits and never taking advantage of what truly belongs to you.

Unfortunately, that is exactly how many of us live after accepting salvation through Jesus. We have been transferred to a new place with new provisions and benefits, yet never learn how to access what belongs to us. In fact, a lot of dear Christians don't believe that they have been set free from lack, sickness, anxiety, depression, and other issues that arise. Worse yet, the devil has lied to people, so they feel that they are not worthy enough to receive good things from God. Well, guess what? Receiving the benefits and blessings of God doesn't hinge on if you are good enough! You could never be good enough because you were made from that "marred with sin" copy. No, you are not good enough, but Jesus was – Praise God! Jesus

> Receiving the benefits and blessings of God doesn't hinge on if you are good enough.

took your sin upon Him and paid for it with His own blood so that you would forever be labeled, "WORTHY!" Now that is a label that you can wear proudly.

My daughter's favorite movie is, "A Knight's Tale." In it, the main character, William, was born a serf but had always wanted to be a knight. He fakes his identity as a knight to be able to compete in jousting tournaments that only can be competed in by those with a royal lineage. He had great success in the competitions but finally is found out and arrested for whom he really is – a serf. Previously during one of his jousting tournaments, he had caught the attention of the Black Prince of Wales (who had also faked his identity so that others would joust with him), and in a very powerful scene, the prince has William released from his shackles and knights him. In that moment, William is transferred from a serf to a knight and grafted into a royal lineage. He not only was named a knight but had the prince's resources and name available to him as well (Helgeland, 2001).

That scene makes me tear up every time I watch it because of the reality of what Christ did for you and me. Jesus provided a true rags-to-riches experience for all who believe on Him. He cleansed us from our sins, giving us a clean slate as well as His name and inheritance.

TOO BLESSED TO BE STRESSED

The Lord's Prayer – how Jesus taught us to pray, says, "...Your will be done on earth AS it is in Heaven" (Matt. 6:9-15). Think about what Heaven is like. I'm sure that it looks a lot different than earth. The Bible says that there is no pain or sickness in heaven. It is a place of abundant blessing. Well, you were transferred into that Kingdom when you asked Jesus to be your Savior – you don't have to wait until you die. I'm here to tell you that the benefits package with salvation is AMAZING and better yet, it is for you and will help you live a life free from depression and anxiety right now.

The concept of God wanting to bless His children may make your brain tilt. Many people have been taught that to be a Christian means to live on "barely-get-by" road. You may have been taught that we just have to deal with the cards we are dealt in life the best we can. You may think that you shouldn't ask God for too much because that is being selfish. However, we are to live like Jesus lived and guess what? Jesus never lacked what He needed. Jesus was so wealthy that He had his own treasurer to keep track of His money. Moreover, He was so wealthy that no one noticed or cared that Judas had been stealing from that account. Jesus' clothes were even so nice that the Roman soldiers cast lots to keep them at His crucifixion.

God isn't against you having things; He is against things having you. He is after your heart, your affection, and your attention. Just like we, as parents, want the best for our children, God wants the best for you too. We strive to provide everything our children need and even desire. God wants to do the same. He wants you whole - spirit, soul, and body - like He intended you to be. Matthew 6:33 is one of my favorite verses about this subject. Jesus says, *"But seek first the kingdom of God and His righteousness, and all these things shall be added to you."* When you seek God, your motives for taking His benefits will be different. Your motive for things will be God-centered instead of me-centered. Once you are able to enjoy the blessings of God, including healing for your soul, you will indeed find that you are too blessed to be stressed.

You are a spirit, you live in a body, and you have a soul. You have been restored and made righteous (which means that you are right with God) and have your citizenship in Heaven. You are of His royal lineage. God declares that you are forgiven, set free, and worthy of all that He has for you.

CHAPTER 2

REFLECTION QUESTIONS

1. Have you had hurtful labels given to you? Or have you talked negatively about yourself? If so, write down those labels that you have maybe started to believe about yourself.

2. What talents or abilities do you possess that you find your identity in?

3. Have you let a relationship determine your identity – either with a friend group or love interest? Even if it's minor, how has your identity changed based on the influence of others?

4. When did you first give your life to Jesus by asking Him into your heart? If you were too young to remember, can you recall when you consciously made a decision to have Christ in your life? Write about that special experience. If you did that for the first time after reading this chapter, write it down and please contact me to let me know.

5. Listen to the song, "Hello, My Name Is" by Matthew West (even if you have heard it a thousand times). What parts of that song can you relate to?

6. You have been given the label of 'Worthy' by God Himself and have been transferred to His Kingdom. Meditate (think on) what that means and how the label of 'Worthy' helps identify who you really are.

chapter three
A NEW WAY OF LIFE |

Our recreated spirit is our real self. It is the part of us that will live forever in Heaven. However, because we are so used to defaulting to the natural part of us (our body and soul), we lack an understanding of the innermost part of our being.

To understand the real you – how you were created, you need to understand the creator Himself. God is probably one of the biggest misunderstood beings ever. It is hard for us to fathom and grasp the depth of who He is. However, the Bible tells us that if we see Jesus, we see the Father. In other words, when we look at the character of Jesus, we will also see the character of God.

GOD IS LOVE

One of the characteristics we can observe about Jesus is that He was very compassionate. Time and time again, the Bible says that He was moved with compassion to heal people and set them free. Well, guess what? He was moved with compassion because God is moved with compassion. Another word for compassion is love – which is who God literally is. God IS love, He doesn't just act in love, but He is the definition of love. 1 Cor. 13:4-8 gives the definition of what love is. You could say that it is God's heart towards us. I am going to put God in the definition so you can see what I mean.

> God is love.
> He doesn't
> just act in
> love, but He is
> the definition
> of love.

"Love (God) endures long and is patient and kind; love (God) never is envious nor boils over with jealousy, (He) is not boastful or vainglorious, (He) does not display itself (Himself) haughtily. Love (God) is not conceited or arrogant and inflated with pride; love (God) is not rude and does not act unbecomingly. Love (God) does not insist on its (His) own rights or its (His) own way, for it (He) is not self-seeking; it (He) is not touchy or fretful or resentful; it (He) takes no account of the evil done to it (Him) — pays no attention to a suffered wrong. Love (God) does not rejoice at injustice and unrighteousness but rejoices when right and truth prevail. Love (God) bears up under anything and everything that comes, it (He) is ever ready to believe the best of every person, Love (God) hopes are fadeless under all circumstances, and it (He) endures everything without weakening. Love (God) never fails, never fades out, or becomes obsolete or comes to an end" (AMPC emphasis mine).

Many times, we have had the picture of God as an angry old man with a big staff ready to thump us on the head when we do something wrong. That is by far the biggest lie of who God is. God is patient with us and is the kindest being you will ever meet.

GOD DOESN'T ALWAYS GET HIS WAY

One of the biggest insights to the character of God and how He operates is in verses 5 and 6…*"Love (God) does not insist on its (His) own rights or its (His) own way…does not rejoice at injustice and unrighteousness, but rejoices when right and truth prevail."* Many people think that God can do anything He wants and that He has control over everything, good and bad. For instance, if a child or a loved one dies, people often say, "God took them because He needed another angel in heaven…" Well, let's take another look at verses 5-6. It says that He "does not insist on His own way." Did you know, just like you and me, that God doesn't always get His way? That would defeat the purpose of giving us a free will. People have choices and often make mistakes or have accidents that were never in God's plan for them. Many times, people die from a sickness or disease because sickness and disease are a part of this world that we live in (part of our marred copy), but that doesn't mean that God wanted nor ever wants sickness to be a part of the human experience.

THE THIEF

John 10:10 gives more insight on the subject. It reads, *"the THIEF comes only in order to STEAL and KILL and DESTROY. I (Jesus) came that they (you) may have and enjoy life, and have it in abundance to the full, till it overflows"* (AMPC emphasis mine).

There is another player in this game of life that people often forget about because he does a great job of shifting the blame for bad things happening from himself to God. The thief, the devil, is a very real and very dangerous foe who wants nothing better than to destroy your life and everyone you love. He does a really good job at making it look like God did it. He whispers things to you like, "If God really loved you, that wouldn't have ever happened to you." Or "God is in control of everything,

> Put the blame where blame is due – on the devil.

so He controlled the sickness too – He used it to teach you something." REALLY?? Would you ever want your child to get sick so he or she learns something? Would you ever send your child to play on the road to get hit by a car so that he or she learns that cars are dangerous? No and No! The Bible says that God is a far better Father than we could ever think of being. He doesn't use evil – He can't or He wouldn't be God.

I want you to use John 10:10 as your guide to know if what you are going through or have experienced is from God or from the devil. If your anxiety stems from something or someone in your life being stolen from you or something that has been destroyed in your life, you can put the blame where blame is due – on the devil.

I know there are a lot of questions here as to why negative circumstances do happen, and that could be a subject for a book in and of itself. What I want you to understand is that God IS love, and He loves you so much and wants only the best for you. He wants your life to be so blessed that it is overflowing with blessing. He loves you so much that He sent Jesus to buy you back with the price of His blood. You are valuable;

> You are valuable, you are worthy, you are not a mistake but are loved by the creator of the whole universe.

you are worthy; you are not a mistake but are loved by the creator of the whole universe. He loves you and cares about everything in your life.

If believing that God loves you is hard for you to grasp, I recommend spending more time with Him. It won't take long for you to experience His love in your life. Another powerful exercise you can do is to look at yourself in the mirror and say OUT LOUD, "God loves me! I am loved by the Most High God, and He cares about me." Then declare to God, "I believe You love me because your Word says You do and You cannot lie. So, I receive that love today!" You may not believe a single word of that when you first start out, but as you continually say it, faith in God and faith in His love for you will grow.

CREATED TO LOVE

As a new creation, you received Jesus in your heart, which put that love on the inside of you. So, not only is 1 Cor. 13 talking about God, but it is also talking about you! You are to walk in that same love – not out of your own ability but out of the Holy Spirit living on the inside of you.

You now have the capacity to be patient and kind toward others through Christ in you. You are not to be envious of others or act conceited or prideful because the love of God is more than enough in your life. You are not to be selfish or touchy – taking offense to people easily. You are not to keep a record and replay injustices done to you (especially with your spouse). We will come back to this one later since that awful replay button in your head will keep anxiety and worry close to you.

I want to end this section with the words from 1 John 4:7-21. It's a bit lengthy, but read it slowly, letting the words really penetrate your heart.

"Dear friends, let us continue to love one another, for love comes from God. Anyone who loves is a child of God and knows God. But anyone who does not love does not know God, for God is love.

God showed how much He loved us by sending His one and only Son into the world so that we might have eternal life through Him. This is real love – not that we loved God, but that He loved us and sent His Son as a sacrifice to take away our sins.

Dear friends, since God loved us that much, we surely ought to love each other. No one has ever seen God. But if we love each other, God lives in us, and His love is brought to full expression in us.

And God has given us His Spirit as proof that we live in Him and He in us. Furthermore, we have seen with our own eyes and now testify that the Father sent His Son to be the Savior of the world. All who declare that Jesus is the Son of God have God living in them, and they live in God. We know how much God loves us, and we have put our trust in His love.

God is love, and all who live in love live in God, and God lives in them. And as we live in God, our love grows more perfect. So we will not be afraid on the day of judgment, but we can face Him with confidence because we live like Jesus here in this world.

Such love has no fear because perfect love expels all fear. If we are afraid, it is for fear of punishment, and this shows that we have not fully experienced His perfect love. We love each other because He loved us first.

If someone says, "I love God," but hates a fellow believer, that person is a liar; for if we don't love people we can see, how can we love God, whom we cannot see? And He has given us this command: Those who love God must also love their fellow believers" (NLT).

CREATED TO LIVE BY FAITH

The Kingdom of God, in which we reside, operates BY faith IN love or through love. Because we cannot tangibly see this Kingdom for now, we must receive it and live in it by faith. We must trust God at His word and trust that the promises in the Bible are true and are for us NOW. For us to trust that the promises and gifts found in the Bible are for us, we must trust in the Giver of those gifts. This goes back to believing His love for us.

Our daughter Callie has always had a special place in her daddy's heart from moment one - and she knew it. When she was two, she knew that he would get up early in the morning to get ready for work and read the Bible. So, she would make sure she was up too. I'm quite certain that she lost a lot of sleep in anticipation of her time with her daddy. She

> We must trust God at His word and trust that the promises in the Bible are true and for us now.

would get up with him and sit on his lap as he ate breakfast and had his morning devotions. She would get her little Bible and "help" him eat his toast. What was she doing? She was building a relationship with him. She never questioned his love for her. She TRUSTED him and TRUSTED his love for her. She trusted that all of her needs would be met – in fact, I'm sure she never even thought about if she would have clothes to wear or food to eat. Now because of this relationship with her dad, she is able to relate to her Father God in the same way. Most importantly, she is able to trust in God for herself and lean on Him to provide her with everything she needs.

You may not have had an earthly father whom you could trust. Maybe you were hurt over and over by your dad or a man close to you. That makes it even harder to develop faith in your heavenly Father and to trust Him with your life. However, just like Callie did with her daddy, the more you spend time with your Father God, the easier it will be to accept His love for you.

RECEIVE IN FAITH

There are many promises in the Bible that are for you to have now – in this lifetime. Salvation didn't just cover your "ticket" to heaven so-to-speak, it covers prosperity and healing as well. Basically, salvation returns us to the way life was before Adam and Eve sinned. They had everything they needed taken care of – and now so do you. However, because this world is so contrary to Eden, you have to receive the prosperity and healing by faith the same way you received your salvation.

Jesus taught about this in Matthew Chapter 6. He basically tells us that you can either trust God to provide for you or trust yourself. I can tell you right now from what I have experienced as a pastor, most people believe in God but don't trust Him to provide for their needs. They love God and have heard that God loves them, but they don't have a true understanding of that love.

> You can either trust God to provide for you or trust yourself.

God wants to meet you where you are. He wants to have an impact on your day-to-day activities from the mundane to the exciting. He has creative ideas, wisdom, and knowledge of how to best handle anything you are dealing with.

Jesus even made the comparison to all of the flowers – how beautifully clothed they are and how God wants to clothe you even better than them. Did you hear that? God likes to shop for you! You think I'm kidding, but I take Him shopping with me all the time. He knows what is going to look best on me and where the best deals are – seriously! He cares about what you care about and wants you to have the best in life. He wants to take care of you and give you all you could hope or imagine. He definitely doesn't want you worrying about those things.

CREATED TO SEEK HIM

The key is to seek Him. As I shared in the previous chapter, Matthew 6:33 says, *"But seek first the kingdom of God and His righteousness, and ALL THESE THINGS shall be added to you. Therefore do not worry about tomorrow, for tomorrow will worry about its own things. Sufficient for the day is its own trouble"* (NKJV emphasis mine). What THINGS is He talking about? He is referring to ALL of the things that you are worrying about, ALL of the things that you care about, and ALL of the things that you need day in and day out.

Hebrews 11:6 adds, *"It's impossible to please God apart from faith. And why? Because anyone who wants to approach God must believe both that he exists and that He cares enough to respond to those who seek Him"* (MSG). There is the key – believing that He cares enough to respond to you. Some people treat God like a genie in a bottle and just ask for things that they think will make them happy. Their heart is not in the right place. The last part of that verse says, "to those who seek Him." Another translation says, "diligently seek" Him. It is a natural transaction when you spend quality time with Him that you will find what you are in need of each and every day. Just like my daughter with her daddy, you won't even question if He will meet your needs because you are so close to Him that all of your needs are met – His 'toast' is your 'toast.' Make a choice to believe that God loves you and cares about you and that He wants to pour His blessings on you to overflowing.

Recently I felt the Lord give me a picture of how most Christians come to Him versus how we should be receiving from our Heavenly Father. Picture a bottle with a narrow opening at the top. The bottle contains the promises of God that belong to you as a believer. Often people come to God, dipping their little finger in the top of the bottle, asking God for just

> **Don't Seek your needs, seek Him.**

one thing - almost afraid to ask too much from Him. They are then disappointed in God when they didn't get what they thought they needed. This type of prayer doesn't, nor will it, get the results you are after. Why? Because maybe there is another issue that needs to be dealt with first. God didn't instruct you to seek the answer to each of your needs individually but to SEEK HIM. When you diligently (which means on a consistent basis, every day) seek Him, it is like if that same bottle unscrewed from the bottom, releasing everything you are in need of at once!

This is how you were created to live - by faith through love. You were created to stay in God's presence and receive what you are in need of on a consistent basis, never lacking any good thing. Psalm 1:1-3 gives another picture of this transaction between God and His people. It reads, *"Oh, the joys of those who do not follow the advice of the wicked, or stand around with sinners, or join in with mockers. But they delight in the law of the Lord, meditating on it day and night. They are like trees planted along the riverbank, bearing fruit each season. Their leaves never wither, and they prosper in all they do" (NLT).*

I believe one of the main reasons that so many people feel lonely and anxious is that they are not trusting God with their lives. They are not planting themselves by the riverbank, which is the love of God. You will continue to experience anxiety at some level when you try to do things on your own. Your spirit is made to rely on and trust in God, to communicate with Him on a regular basis, and to experience a life of love and peace.

Just the practice of talking to God on a regular (all day long) basis will cause anxiety to subside. Start by vocalizing your love and trust in Him – yes, out loud. Declare that you are loved by God and don't let any idea contrary to that sneak into your thoughts.

Find some quality time to spend with your Father God without other distractions. Find a time that you can "crawl up on His lap and eat His toast" (the Word of God). Go for a walk, take a bubble bath, or get up before anyone else to sit and get to know your creator. Start with reading a scripture and meditating on it. Ask God to reveal Himself to you on a deeper level than you have experienced before. There isn't one person on the face of the planet who has even scratched the surface of knowing and experiencing the depths of God's love. Don't feel like you have to have a doctorate in theology to have a conversation with God. In fact, Jesus told His disciples to be more like children when coming to Him. Simply believe that He loves and cares about you and that He wants the very best for you.

CHAPTER 3

REFLECTION QUESTIONS

1. After reading 1 Corinthians 13:4-8, what part of that definition of who God is resonates with you the most? Which part surprised you the most?

2. How have you personally viewed God? Have you ever blamed Him for something bad in your life?

3. Do you believe that God loves you? Write yourself a love note from God in your journal. Let Him speak to your heart as you write.

4. Does putting your full trust in God make you nervous? Are there parts of your life that you haven't fully trusted Him with? List those areas and spend time praying over them, ask God to help you give each of those things over to Him.

5. In your quiet time with God, revisit the scriptures from this chapter. Focus on one passage at a time, asking God to speak to you through His Word. Journal anything that you feel God is speaking to you about.

chapter four

IT'S A SOUL THING |

The realm of your soul is where we will give much of our attention concerning breaking free from stress and anxiety. Your soul contains three parts. The first part is your mind, which includes your thoughts, reasoning, and imagination. The second part is your will, which is the fortitude and determination to stick with something. The last part is your emotions, which is how you feel at any given time. All of these areas are very complex and tough to sort out, which is why anxiety and other mental illnesses are such difficult things to get a handle on.

Your soul is an amazingly complicated part of who you are. It is the 'middleman' so-to-speak that connects to your spirit as well as to your body. The soul receives information from the physical realm through the five physical senses; yet, at the same time, the soul can communicate with the center of who you are - your spirit. A mother's intuition is an example of this communication in action. We call it a "gut reaction" or just a "knowing."

HEARING GOD'S VOICE

This is also the way that we hear God speaking to us. God speaks to your spirit, which is 'translated' to your mind so that you can understand. You may have wondered, "Is this really God that I am hearing, or is it my own thoughts?" Well, you are hearing God speak to you from your spirit, but it is filtered through your soul - in your voice so that you can understand. Very rarely do people hear the audible voice of God.

So, how do you know if it's God speaking or just your own thoughts?

Well, the first way to recognize His voice is to read the Bible. God will never contradict His Word. If what you are feeling contradicts what the Bible says in any way (loneliness, fear, depression, or anxiety), then it is not God speaking to you. The fruit of the Spirit – which comes from God, is love, joy, peace, patience, kindness, goodness, faithfulness, gentleness, and self-control (Galatians 5:22-23). Hearing from God will always fall under the banner of love. He will not condemn you, ridicule you, or hold any of your sins over your head. Those voices and thoughts are straight from the father of lies, Satan.

WHAT DO YOU BELIEVE?

Your soul contains your foundational beliefs, which can be influenced by many things. There is a quote by Gandhi that actually rings very true. He said:

> Your beliefs become your thoughts,
> Your thoughts become your words,
> Your words become your actions,
> Your actions become your habits,
> Your habits become your values,
> Your values become your destiny.

The reverse is also true; your life, what you are experiencing right now is a result of what you value in your life, what you value in your life has come from your habits, your habits have come from your actions, your actions from your words, and your words from what you truly believe.

For example, let's take the idea of exercise. Those who don't exercise typically don't because they don't value it, and because they don't value it, it has not become a habit in their lives. Of course, we know that a habit can't be formed without doing it for a period of time. That lack of action probably stemmed from complaining about exercise, saying that they just don't like it or that they can't do it for some reason. Those words came from thoughts – thoughts about what they *think* about themselves or what they *think* others *think* of them (that's a lot of thinking) or their thoughts of exercise itself. Those thoughts came from their belief about exercise or even their belief about themselves.

HEALTHY SOUL = HEALTHY LIFE

John understood how important the health of your soul is as he wrote 3 John 2, *"Beloved, I pray that you may prosper in all things and be in health, just as your soul prospers."* Do you see how this verse is like an equation? The word, "AS," operates like an equal sign. This means that your health and prosperity (in every area of your life) is directly tied to and related to

> **If your mental health is good than your life will be good.**

the health of your soul. Again, your soul includes your mind, will, and emotions. If your mental health is good, then your life is good. If your mental health is bad, then your life is going to be… not what it should or could be.

Anxiety definitely reveals itself in many ways, including the health of your physical body. Although I thought I was outwardly concealing my anxiety and panic attacks, it popped out in little things that I did. For instance, I would rub my earrings or ear lobes without thinking about it. I would play with my hair, running my fingers through it over and over again. I would clench my jaw and probably do other little things that I wasn't even aware of. The anxiety that I experienced leaked out into all the parts of my body. It even caused me to gain weight and made it harder to lose weight.

As I am sure you are aware, every aspect of your life is negatively affected by anxiety. Relationships with your spouse, kids, co-workers, and friends all reap the ramifications of the health of your soul – good or bad. Have you ever noticed that when you feel good, it seems that everyone treats you better? People smile at you and are friendly. However, when you feel negative, it seems as though everyone is upset with you and 'out to get you.' The reason this seems to be the case is that we see others through the lens of our own soul, which tints our perspective on any given situation.

THOUGHTS AND FEELINGS

Your thoughts are very powerful. I remember as a child being intrigued by the notion that I could think whatever I wanted, and no one knew those thoughts but myself. That realization was very powerful to a quiet, introverted little girl. Although I was very obedient and compliant in my actions, I could be as defiant as I wanted on the inside without any consequence. No one was going to judge me even if I was wrong. I was, indeed, correct in the fact that my thoughts are very powerful. I was also right in the fact that no one has to know what I am thinking. That is a skill that can be a good thing but at the same time a very troubling problem because a lot of us have gotten very proficient at putting smiles on our faces when we are anything but smiling on the inside. That is exactly what high-functioning anxiety looks like, and it is a lie!

Now I will add that it is a very good practice not to say everything we think. There are a lot of thoughts that run through our heads during the day, many of which will not benefit anyone if spoken or written on social media. People often just say whatever is on their minds and don't care what anyone thinks about their words or if they hurt others. That is also very wrong. We are to walk in love, being kind to one another. Saying what you want so that you 'feel' better even though it might hurt someone else is selfish, immature and sinful.

We are not to be ruled by our feelings but instead by our recreated spirits. Our feelings are very fickle. They can be high one minute and low the next. They can be controlled by what we eat, the amount of sleep we get, our hormones, or any other outside stimulus. Many times, our feelings lie to us about how things really are. They are selfish and see situations one-sided and are often wrong. Have you ever let a bad moment or incident ruin your whole day? I know I have! If you let your feelings dictate to you how your day is going, then you better buckle up for a bumpy, crazy ride! Your emotions can have you on a high one moment and without notice, send you crashing to a low.

The other day I witnessed a little scenario with my middle school students when two girls left the little group they were standing in to go walk around. Immediately when they left, I overheard one of the students remaining in the group say, "I bet they're talking about us." Observing the situation, I highly doubt that was true at all. However, the fear of being rejected at that age is so high that any actions of others that could give a hint to validate those feelings of insecurity and rejection seem true and real.

Following your feelings will derail the plan of God for your life. Your feelings will tell you to take the easy way, hold a grudge, sit on the couch and binge watch TV, eat that pint of ice cream, give someone a piece of your mind, or even date someone and give yourself to that person because of lust or a shallow feeling of acceptance. Think about how each of those little decisions to follow your feelings could cause havoc in your life. You have probably seen on the news when an incident of road rage (which started with a small incident) ends up costing someone's life. This happens as a result of letting thoughts and feelings rule one's life.

THINK ABOUT WHAT YOU ARE THINKING ABOUT

Your soul is the part of you that holds all of your memories and imagination. This means you can do a lot of thinking about the past and the future. Your imagination is an amazing thing when used how God intended it. You can dream of the future and see yourself successful. You have the power to picture yourself living your best life. In fact, that is faith in action – seeing yourself successful before actually experiencing that success.

The devil, however, also has access to your thoughts and will do whatever he can to hold you in bondage to your past and push you to worry about the future. If you choose to take those negative thoughts that he feeds you and dwell on them, he will camp out and keep feeding you worry after worry, lie after lie. The good news is YOU have the authority to take back your thoughts and to send the devil fleeing from you.

You don't have to hold on to every thought that comes into your head. What you think about is your choice. It has been scientifically proven that you can erase negative (toxic) thoughts and recreate healthy thoughts that line up with the Word of God. I highly recommend reading Dr. Caroline Leaf's books on the subject. She has dedicated her life to the study of neuroscience and showing how these Bible truths are proven scientifically.

I love what Paul writes in Philippians 4:6-8 concerning your thought life. He says, *"Do not fret or have any anxiety about anything, but in every circumstance and in everything, by prayer and petition (definite requests), with thanksgiving, continue to make your wants known to God.*

And God's peace shall be yours, that tranquil state of a soul assured of its salvation through Christ, and so fearing nothing from God and being content with its earthly lot of whatever sort that is, that peace which transcends all understanding shall garrison and mount guard over your hearts and minds in Christ Jesus.

For the rest, brethren, whatever is true, whatever is worthy of reverence and is honorable and seemly, whatever is just, whatever is pure, whatever is lovely and lovable, whatever is kind and winsome and gracious, if there is anything worthy of praise, think on and weigh and take account of these things – fix your minds on them" (AMPC).

To achieve that "tranquil state" of your soul, you are going to have to get tough about what you think about. Thinking on wrong things doesn't just stay in your mind but leaks out into your body and what you say and do. If the devil can get you thinking on wrong thoughts and get you to believe those things, they can actually become reality in your life.

Remember in chapter 1, I said that I let thoughts take root in my mind and made a conscious decision to think about wrong things? Well, for a time, especially when my kids were young, I would think about what would happen if my husband or one of my children died. I know, morbid! I would rehearse scenarios about what I would do, where I would live, and if I would remarry. I even rehearsed how I would feel to the point that it brought me to tears. I want to say right here that if you think those kinds of thoughts, you need to stop immediately. Those thoughts were not just innocent thoughts of preparing for what-ifs. Using John 10:10 as a guide – the thief comes to steal, kill, and destroy, I knew that those thoughts were not from God.

This is how the enemy works because he knows that if he can get you to think about something long enough, you will begin to believe that it can or even will happen. If you believe that something bad is going to happen, you will begin to talk that way, and that is when the devil snares you. I let the fear of those thoughts take root so that I had to fight back fear of death every time my husband or I traveled apart from each other. If I hadn't gotten control of those toxic thoughts by giving them to God and resisting the urge to think along those lines, I'm sure I would have gotten to the point of having too much anxiety even to leave my home.

Let's go back to Philippians 4:6-8 to learn what should be filling our minds. First, he says to think about whatever is true. Well, right there knocks out much of what fills our thoughts. Have you ever heard the acronym for fear being - **F**alse **E**vidence, **A**ppearing **R**eal? The devil works really hard to make things seem real when, in actuality, they are anything but the truth.

F alse
E vidence
A ppearing
R eal

Next, we are to think about whatever is worthy of reverence and is honorable. If you have been falsely accused of something or bad-mouthed, don't think on it. "What?" You may be saying, "How do you not think about something like that?" Well, if it is true, then you have some repenting to do to clear it up, but if it is false, then it isn't worth your time. You are not going to change anything by dwelling on it. It only has power over you if you give it the power.

TAKE YOUR THOUGHTS CAPTIVE

The Bible says in 2 Corinthians 10:5, "*We demolish arguments and every pretension that sets itself up against the knowledge of God, and we take captive every thought to make it obedient to Christ*" *(NIV)*. Do you see what YOU have the power to do? YOU can demolish thoughts and take them captive from residing in your mind.

I didn't even know about this verse when I first discovered that I had control over my thoughts. As a young girl, I would have a recurring nightmare. I hated this nightmare and didn't want to have it anymore. So, I found out that I could control my dreams (take my thoughts captive). When I started having that nightmare, I took control and made myself the hero of my dream. After doing that, I never had that nightmare again. Side note: I taught my children that they had the ability to do that as well. As a result of learning the truth about their thoughts, they too took control of their nightmares.

James 4:7 says, "*Submit yourselves, then, to God* (what God says about you in the Bible). *Resist the devil* (and the negative thoughts that he gives you) *and he will flee from you* (NKJV emphasis mine). You don't have to accept those wrong thoughts as truth. Just like you can return a package that you don't want by returning it to the sender, you can return those negative thoughts to the sender as well!

CHANGE YOUR MIND

You not only have control over your thoughts, but science has now proven that you can actually change the chemical make-up of your mind. In other words, you have the ability to change your brain's wiring. It is what the Bible refers to as: renewing your mind. Renewing your mind God's way does just that – gives you a NEW mind, a new way of thinking and acting. You can slowly be transformed to be physically and spiritually anxiety free.

Romans 12:1-2 says, *"Therefore I urge you, brothers and sisters, by the mercies of God, to present your bodies dedicating all of yourselves, set apart as a living sacrifice, holy and well-pleasing to God, which is your rational (logical, intelligent) act of worship. And do not be conformed to this world any longer with its superficial values and customs, but be transformed and progressively changed as you mature spiritually by the renewing of your mind focusing on godly values and ethical attitudes, so that you may prove for yourselves what the will of God is, that which is good and acceptable and perfect in His plan and purpose for you"* (AMPC).

God has provided all you need to receive healing in your mind. You see, when you asked Jesus into your heart, your spirit man (the real you) was recreated, and immediately, you became righteous – having right standing with God. Your eternal home was moved from Hell to Heaven in a moment.

Salvation is the *easy* part for us. We just have to receive Jesus and believe that He died on the cross for us. However, your body and mind were not recreated at the same point in which you were saved. That is why you still act and talk like you did before you asked Jesus into your heart. It is your choice to renew your mind and present your body as a living sacrifice. Paul, who is the writer of Romans, was urging Christians to go a step

> **It is your choice to renew your mind and present your body as a living sacrifice.**

further than just getting into heaven. He encouraged believers to renew their minds with the Word of God for a total transformation.

Many Christians stay in the 'shallow' end of Christianity. They have received salvation, but there is no change in the rest of their lives. Why? Because disciplining the mind and body is NO FUN! We are to present ourselves as a LIVING SACRIFICE. Sacrifice means it will cost you something, but trust me: the trade -off is well worth it! A disciplined life will create your best life. However, the only way to have a disciplined life is to transform your thinking, which will, in turn, transform your actions and habits. Being self-disciplined will change your life because the only one who can really prevent you from reaching your dreams and your best life is you!

Paul writes in Romans 12:1 that dedicating your body and what you do on a daily basis to God is pleasing to Him because it is an act of worship. It is placing God in the #1 position in every area of your life. In other words, God is helping me be the best wife I can be; He's giving me wisdom on how to parent my children, He's giving me creative ideas in my job and showing me how to have meaningful relationships with those around me. I am allowing Him to speak to me about every area of my life. He even cares about my hobbies and what I do to relax.

He wants to be involved in everything you do, and why not? HE MADE YOU. I know it blesses me when my teen-age kids ask for my input or my help or just want to spend time with me. God is the same way. He loves you and wants to spend time with you. Really!

When you allow God to speak to you about your life, He will. However, you still have the choice whether or not to listen to Him and submit your will to His. His way will take effort. It will take laying down your ideas and being self-disciplined to change the way you have previously acted and previously thought. The scripture says that His thoughts are higher than your thoughts and His ways are higher than your ways (Isaiah 55:8-9). That means that His way of dealing with issues that arise in your life is going to be different than you may be used to.

Problems arise when you use natural remedies to deal with your soul issues instead of calling on the help of the Holy Spirit. For example, you might go to the bar to take your mind off of things, or you might reach for that pint of ice cream when you're feeling sad. By doing that, you are turning to natural remedies to help with your SOUL problems. You might feel good for the moment, but I guarantee most of the time those short-term remedies will cause your problems to get bigger. Having a drink every time you need to take your mind off of problems could lead you down a path of alcoholism. Turning to food for comfort will create health problems and eventually self-esteem issues due to the excess weight gain. Instead, spend time in prayer to take your mind off of stressful situations. Read the Word or listen to uplifting Praise and Worship music when you are feeling sad. Find friends who are positive and will support your new lifestyle of relying on God.

An amazing thing happens when you continually turn to God's Word for wisdom in every situation. Your mind will become renewed. When your mind is renewed to the Word of God, you will find that your stress and anxiety will diminish and, in its place, will be a peace that passes your understanding. It doesn't mean that your problems will disappear overnight, but it does mean that those things won't impact you negatively because now you have wisdom to deal with situations that come your way.

FIND YOUR FOUNDATION

Your soul is just like a house that needs a good foundation to be built on. In the story of the three little pigs, the big bad wolf came to each house, no matter what it was made out of. The pigs that were hasty about building their houses out of sticks and hay paid the price later. However, the pig that chose to build his house with bricks didn't mind when the wolf came because he had made for himself a place of fortitude. He spent time building something that would withstand outside pressures.

So many times, people want the quick fixes that the first little pigs demonstrated; however, when hardships come, they fall to the elements of the pressure. Renewing your mind to the things of God will strengthen your fortitude so that when the 'big bad wolves of life' come (and they will), you will go unscathed.

Jesus actually told the original *Three Little Pigs* story in the Bible. Check out Matthew 7:24-27; in it, Jesus talks about the wise man who built his house upon the rock. The rain and wind (storms of life) came to him just the same as to everyone else, but the house stayed firm on that rock. The rock that He was speaking of is the Word of God. It is the firm foundation that you need under you to withstand the storms of life. He also told of what happened when another man built his house on his own ideals – his own way, independent from God. When the storms came, the Bible says that his house didn't just fall, but GREAT was its fall.

You may require a little demolition of your thinking before you can start to rebuild the life that God intended for you. Let the Holy Spirit start to speak to you about changes you need to make to get your foundation set correctly.

ACTION STEPS

Make reading the Word a priority in your life. Just as you need to shower and brush your teeth every day, your mind needs to be *washed* with the Word every day. At times, it is good for us to do a food cleanse to get rid of all the garbage in our digestive system. It is just as important to do a spiritual cleanse. For a designated time, totally submerge yourself in the Word. That means instead of watching mindless TV and listening to secular music, listen and watch Christian music and programming. The VICTORY network is an awesome resource for this. You can find it on YouTube, Roku, or on DISH. Listen to praise and worship music while you sleep or work. Read other books like this one to help in your Christian walk and learn how to live a victorious life.

Don't let your mind take you hostage another day but break free by taking your thoughts captive. Replace those negative thoughts and feelings with the Word and what God says about you.

CHAPTER 4

REFLECTION QUESTIONS

1. When was the last time that you really felt God speaking to you? Practice hearing the voice of God. Write down what you feel He is speaking to you.

2. On a scale from 1-5, with 1 being poor and 5 being great, rate the health of your soul right now. How does that honest rating correlate to the health of your life?

3. How have your feelings and emotions lied to you about who you are? Let yourself imagine that you are living your best life possible. What does that look like and feel like?

4. Identify thoughts that you have that are fear-based. Take time to write them out. Now speak 2 Cor. 10:5 over them. Say, "I demolish these evil thoughts in the Name of Jesus and purpose to take my thoughts captive to the obedience of Christ!"

5. What things have you used to cope with anxiety and/or depression? What has been the result of those actions?

chapter five

FAITH VS. FEAR |

The fight of the ages is between these two opponents right here – Faith VS Fear. Faith and fear are direct opposites of each other and are both vying for your attention. Faith simply believes what God says is true, whereas fear believes the lies that the devil twists to *seem* true. Faith and fear cannot coincide at the same time. You either line up with God and His Word, or you unknowingly line up with Satan and his lies.

> **Faith simply believes what God says is true.**

The definition of faith is found in Hebrews 11:1. It says, *"Now faith is the reality of what is hoped for, the proof of what is not seen" (CSB)*. That simply means that faith pulls the promises of God from the spiritual realm (unseen) into the natural realm (seen). It causes the Good News of the Bible to be more than words on a page but a reality in your life.

Using faith is similar to a fisherman reeling in his catch. When he first puts his bait and line into the water, he is *hoping* for a fish. If he is really good at fishing, he is even *expecting* to catch that fish. That fisherman is so confident that when a fish bites, he is not surprised by it but calmly starts reeling it in a little at a time – especially a big fish. In fact, the bigger the catch, the more patient the fisherman has to be to bring that fish from the murky waters into the boat.

Faith is like that fishing pole. It is used to "reel in" the promises in the Word from the unseen (something you are not experiencing right now) to the seen (physical realm). Just like the fisherman, using your faith requires patience as well.

Fear works the same way. Fear is worrying about your life and those you care about and actually putting your faith in negative circumstances happening in your life. It's expecting to reel in weeds instead of a fish!

SPIRITUAL LAW

There are laws that govern the spirit realm, just like there are laws that govern the physical realm. For instance, the law of gravity works for everyone, no matter your age, nationality, location, or your belief in God. The law demands that what goes up must come down. Even an airplane that seems to defy the law of gravity with the law of lift will eventually come down if it runs out of fuel. There is no escaping the law of gravity anywhere on the face of this planet.

> **Until you speak to the anxiety and depression taking residence in your soul, you will never break free from its bondage.**

The same is true for the spiritual law of attraction using the power of your words. Since the beginning of time, words carry a creative force that when spoken, carry out what was said. Take a look at Genesis 1:1, *"In the beginning God created the heavens and the earth. The earth was without form, and void; and darkness was on the face of the deep. And the Spirit of God was hovering over the face of the waters. Then God SAID, 'Let there be light; and there was light"* (NKJV emphasis mine).

The rest of what God created follows the same pattern. God said it and then it happened. He didn't just say it because He felt like it – no! He spoke it because that is the spiritual law of creation. This law is to be a blessing to us. It is actually how we were designed to function because we are made in the image of God. Some people refer to this supernatural law as the law of attraction, meaning that what you focus on and talk about is what will become a reality in your life.

You can find story after story of celebrities such as Jim Carrey, Steve Harvey, and Oprah Winfrey, who beat the odds against them and made their dreams a reality by following this spiritual principle. I'm not sure they even knew it was a spiritual law that they were putting into practice. Nevertheless, they imagined what they wanted in life and began speaking that success before anyone knew their names. Soon their words became a reality!

We are also greatly affected by words spoken to us or about us. When I was younger, I was a bit chunky. I remember distinctively a boy (I didn't even know) asking my brother, "Is that fat girl your sister?" I had never been called fat before and never was called fat again, but those words struck me hard. During those wonderful puberty years, I went from 5'4" and 145 lbs. to 5'6" and 110 lbs. I was very skinny, but because I had been labeled as fat, I couldn't see myself any other way. When I would see pictures of myself, I couldn't believe that that was actually me. I am very fortunate that my frame of mind, due to one single sentence spoken, didn't send me into an eating disorder.

SPEAK TO YOUR MOUNTAIN

Mark 11:22-24 says, *"So Jesus answered and said to them, 'Have faith in God. For assuredly, I say to you, whoever says to this mountain, be removed and be cast into the sea, and does not doubt in his heart, but believes that those things he says will be done, he will have whatever he says. Therefore, I say to you, whatever things you ask when you pray, believe that you receive them, and you will have them."*

The first direction Jesus gives is, "Have faith in God." This statement is simple yet hard for many of us to do. God has to have **your** faith in Him to perform His Word for you. Hebrews 11:6 says, *"But without faith it is impossible to please Him (God), for he who comes to God must believe that He is, and that He is a rewarder of those who diligently seek Him" (NKJV emphasis mine).* Becoming a Christian requires the action of believing in Him – trusting in Him and confessing that He is your Lord and Savior. The same first step used to come to God is also the first step in receiving anything from Him – Have faith and believe that His word is true.

> God has to have your faith in Him to perform His Word for you.

The next step that Jesus instructs His disciples to do (as well as us) in Mark 11:22-23 is to SPEAK to the mountain. *"For assuredly, I say to you, whoever SAYS to this mountain."* The mountain Jesus is speaking of is both literal and figurative. Figuratively the mountain refers to any problem you are facing. Better yet, it is referring to any problem that you are facing that He has told you in His word that you don't have to put up with – i.e., anxiety. How do you learn what things you don't have to put up with? You know the answer, READ THE WORD! How do you know what belongs to you or what doesn't belong to you if you have never read your manual – which also contains your benefits package of salvation? Reading the word will help you to recognize the *mountains* in your life that you should be getting rid of by faith.

Many people are waiting around for God to take their *mountain* from them while they wallow in their circumstances, doubting that God really loves them. However, God loves you and cares about you so much that He sent His son to die for you – to gain the victory for you. All you have to do is learn how to receive it. Jesus is instructing us on how to receive those promises from God and how to reject the problems of this world and the devil through our words. Notice he didn't say to think the mountain away or hope it goes away. No, He said SPEAK to it – OUT LOUD. You might be thinking, "Well, I would feel silly doing that!" My answer to that is: Go ahead and keep your problems then because until you learn to speak to your problems and declare God's word over your life, your circumstances will never change. Until you speak to the anxiety and depression taking residence in your soul, you will never break free from its bondage.

There is an account in Jesus' ministry that is recorded to show us the powerful reality of fear vs. faith. It begins in Mark 5:21, *"Now when Jesus had crossed over again by boat to the other side, a great multitude gathered to Him; and He was by the sea. And behold one of the rulers of the synagogue came, Jairus by name. And when he saw Him, he fell at His feet and begged Him earnestly, saying, 'My little daughter lies at the point of death. Come and lay Your hands on her, that she may be healed, and she will live'."*

Jesus is approached by Jairus to come heal his little girl who is almost dead. The first thing to point out here is that he didn't doubt that Jesus could or would do it. Why? He had heard about Jesus and believed that He could heal his daughter. Romans 10:1 says, *"faith comes by hearing, and hearing by the word of God."* This means that he had heard about Jesus, and as he

> If the thief comes to steal it, Jesus comes to heal it!

heard about Him and what He did for others, his faith in Jesus grew. He believed that Jesus could heal his daughter. This will work the exact same way for you. Reading the word and listening to faith-filled sermons and messages will build your faith in God without fail. Faith is like a muscle - we all have faith, but your faith will become strengthened by reading the word (just like doing exercises will strengthen your body). The second thing to point out is that Jairus recognized that sickness and death are not of God – again remember John 10:10, *"The thief does not come except to steal, and to kill, and to destroy..."* If the thief comes to steal it, Jesus comes to heal it!

Verses 24 goes on to say, *"So Jesus went with him, and a great multitude followed Him and thronged Him."* I want you to get the picture of what is going on here. Jairus is elated that he got Jesus to come to his house. However, people began recognizing Jesus and came from every direction to see him. The scene reminds me of when a famous rock band or a celebrity is recognized in public, and all of a sudden, a mob of fans gather around them wanting to touch them and get their autographs and a picture. However, people wanted much more than an autograph from Jesus; they were desperate for healing and deliverance.

The event continues, as distractions seem to get in the way. Verse 25 – *"Now a certain woman had a flow of blood for twelve years and had suffered many things from many physicians. She had spent all that she had and was no better, but rather grew worse. When she heard about Jesus, she came behind Him in the crowd and touched His garment. For she said, 'If only I may touch His clothes, I shall be made well.' Immediately the fountain of her blood was dried up, and she felt in her body that she was healed of the affliction. And Jesus, immediately knowing in Himself that power had gone out of Him, turned around in the crowd and said, 'Who touched My clothes?' But His disciples said to Him, 'You see the multitude thronging You, and You say, 'Who touched Me?'' And He looked around to see her who had done this thing. But the woman, fearing and trembling, knowing what had happened to her, came and fell down before Him and told Him the whole truth. And He said to her, 'Daughter, your faith has made you well. Go in peace, and be healed of your affliction.'"*

This woman shows us faith in action. She demonstrates what faith looks like, what faith sounds like, and what faith acts like. She had done everything she knew to do by going to doctors to try to get better, but nothing they did helped. In fact, they made her condition worse! I thank God for doctors; they are in the same business as Jesus – healing. However, sometimes, a doctor is limited to how much they can help a patient. On the contrary, Jesus is never limited! If you have struggled with an ailment that has continually gotten worse, be like this woman and believe that Jesus will heal you. This woman heard about Jesus just like Jairus, and just like Jairus, her faith in Jesus grew. Not only did her faith grow, but she also matched her words to her faith – verse 28, "For she SAID…" She activated the faith that was growing on the inside of her by speaking the desired outcome – "I shall be made well." That is a bold statement, but true faith is bold! It looks adversity in the face and says, "I don't think so! Jesus took my infirmity upon Himself, so I don't have to put up with it – I believe and declare by faith in Jesus' Name that by His stripes I am healed and set free!"

Notice Jesus wasn't even paying attention to the woman with the issue of blood – He was focused on Jairus. Yet, He stopped when He felt power had gone out of Him. How cool is that? HER faith activated the healing power of Jesus; HER faith stopped Jesus in His tracks – even when she didn't want the attention. She wasn't supposed to be in public with this kind of blood issue. In fact, she could have been stoned for being there. But she strengthened her faith, and there was nothing (not even death) that was going to stop her from receiving her healing – now that is a determined person! Notice what Jesus said to her, "YOUR faith made you well." Why? Because that is the way the kingdom operates. Your words in line with God's Word activates the power of God to work on your behalf. It's just like turning on a light switch. The power is constantly there to make the light turn on, but it takes YOU physically flipping the switch to activate that power. Faith-filled words operate like a switch that will turn on the power of God in your life.

> Your words in line with God's Word, activates the power of God to work on your behalf.

We will pick up this event in verse 35. It says, *"While He (Jesus) was still speaking, some came from the ruler of the synagogue's house who said, 'Your daughter is dead. Why trouble the Teacher any further?' As soon as Jesus heard the word that was spoken, He said to the ruler of the synagogue, 'Do not be afraid; only believe.'"*

Again, we can learn a great deal from Jesus' response to the bad news. I believe He was very stern when He gave Jairus the order, "Do not fear, only believe." It is important for you to realize that Jesus could not have done anything for Jairus' daughter if Jairus would have chosen to turn off his faith and instead follow his feelings of fear. Faith is like a key that you give Jesus to have access to your circumstance. On the other hand, when you are in fear or worry, you have unknowingly just handed the keys to the devil to have access to your situation. That is a serious thought.

> **Faith is like a key that you give Jesus to have access to your circumstance.**

If you read the rest of the event, Jairus stayed in faith and Jesus healed the little girl. However, Jesus did have to put those who were grieving for the girl outside of the house before He could do anything. He couldn't have their doubt "infecting" and ultimately affecting the outcome. When you are dealing with a situation in your own life and standing in faith, you may have to distance yourself from those who don't have the same faith as you do for a little while. They may have great intentions, but you can't afford to let your faith get contaminated with their doubt.

THE POWER OF YOUR WORDS

Your words are powerful – more powerful than you realize. Proverbs 18:21 says, *"Death and life are in the power of the tongue."* Wow – that is quite the statement. Because we were made in the image of God, we operate like God, meaning our words are powerful just like God's Words are powerful. The devil knows that is how we are made and doesn't care if you don't understand it or didn't mean what you said, he will use it against you anyway. You see, when you start speaking the negative thoughts that he has planted, he can bring those fears into reality. Don't let false, fear-based words out of your mouth.

WATCH WHAT YOU SAY

What you give your attention to and talk about is what will come about - just like the woman with the issue of blood. Think about what you have been saying and giving your attention to. Do you want those things coming true in your life? If not, start confessing the right things. Speak victory over your life. For example:

- "I am healed from anxiety in Jesus' name."
- "I am happy and full of joy."
- "I have a happy and healthy marriage." (even if you're not married yet)
- "I am an overcomer."
- "I enjoy life and have good success."
- "The favor and blessing of the Lord follow me wherever I go."

If you start speaking those positive confessions over your life in faith, you are guaranteed to find yourself in a place of success and peace. The key to all of this is that you must stay in contact with God - letting His Word work in you. He is the source that an abundant life comes from.

Isn't it awesome that God doesn't leave us to fight our battles by ourselves unarmed? He has also given us the armor of God to be victorious in any battle we face. Ephesians chapter 6:10-20 describes each piece of armor that God has given us to fight our battles. I'm not going to go into each part of the armor; there are great books written with in-depth studies on the armor of God. I do want to point out, however, that God has given us an amazing offensive weapon. You have been entrusted to use the sword of the Spirit, which is the Word of God (Ephesians 6:17). A sword in the hands of a skilled fighter is designed to kill anyone or anything that comes its way.

God wants you to be a skilled fighter. You become skilled by knowing what the Bible says and using the Word of God to strike blow after blow to the enemy. You ought to be so skilled in the Word that the Devil flees from you in terror when you wake up in the morning!

It takes strength to wield such a powerful sword, and God provided that as well. The Bible says in Nehemiah 8:10, *"...the joy of the Lord is your strength.*" Philippians 4:4 also declares, *"Rejoice in the Lord always, Again I will say, rejoice!"* You might be thinking, "but I don't feel like rejoicing." This type of rejoicing doesn't come from a feeling. You can rejoice because faith says you already have the victory. Furthermore, while you are rejoicing, you are getting stronger and will be able to withstand the attacks from the enemy. Did you know that your body can't tell the difference between a fake laugh and a real laugh? So, start to laugh on purpose – HA HA HA! It won't take long for your feelings to catch up and for strength to come to you.

The winner of the battles in your life is totally up to you. Yes, I did say the plural "battles." When the children of Israel were given the Promised Land, they had to fight battle after battle for it. They had big enemies that they had to conquer. However, God was with them and fighting for them every step of the way. You have battles to fight to enter into your promised land, but the good news is, Jesus already got the victory for you – you just have to walk it out. Don't try and fight your battles alone. Get plugged into a good church and surround yourself with like-minded believers who will pray for you and come alongside you in your battles.

The winner of the battle between faith and fear is ultimately up to you. Will you listen to fear and continue to speak worry and doubt in your life, or will you choose to let faith be victorious by siding with what God says in His Word? Like I said, victory IS yours when you speak the Word of God over your life and situations. Psalm 68:1 declares, *"Let God arise, Let His enemies be scattered."* Let God arise mightily in you through faith!

CHAPTER 5

REFLECTION QUESTIONS

1. Do you tend to expect positive or negative outcomes in your life? Are there certain issues that you are more fearful of? Why do you think that is?

2. Identify "mountains" in your life that are hindering you. Remember to use John 10:10 as your guide. If it is stealing from you, killing you, or destroying your life, it is a mountain that needs to be dealt with.

3. How developed do you feel your "faith muscle" is? How are you hearing the Word? Identify any hindrances that prevent you from strengthening your faith.

4. What you talk about is what will come about. Write out the declarations that I gave in this chapter. Now write out some personal declarations that you want to see come to pass in your life.

5. You gain strength for your battles through joy. Go back to the list of "mountains" you identified. Now laugh at each one and declare a positive outcome over them.

chapter six
LIVE IN THE NOW |

Now that you have a foundational understanding about how you were created and how faith and fear are both competing for your words, you can start to put that knowledge to work. There is another component to faith that is also very important in regard to demolishing anxiety issues.

Hebrews 11:1 says, *"NOW faith is the substance of things hoped for, the evidence of things not seen"* (NKJV emphasis mine). Faith is NOW. It doesn't wish things would be different in the future but believes NOW that things ARE different - before the change even occurs.

Most of our thoughts are consumed with scenarios we have little control over today. We worry about how to pay for college, how we are going to do on a test, how a tough conversation will go, where we will live, our spouse, kids' futures, what people think about us, and the list goes on and on. All of these things take up precious space in our minds. What do you think would happen if all of those uncontrollable issues about the future or the past were erased from your thinking? Would anything about today change? The answer is no!

Jesus instructed us in Matthew 6:11 to pray for THIS day – "give us this day our daily bread." In the Old Testament, God gave the children of Israel manna from heaven DAILY. They were instructed to gather the manna each day – just for that day. Yesterday's manna was gone and thinking about it wasn't going to fill them up today. They were to eat all of the manna daily. In fact, if any of the manna was left over, it bred worms and stank. That is the same thing that happens when you dwell on a negative past issue – it breeds worms of unforgiveness and stinks up your life.

DO NOT WORRY ABOUT TOMORROW

Jesus continued to teach on this subject of worry and anxiety saying in Matthew 6:34, *"Do not worry about tomorrow, for tomorrow will worry about its own things."* Notice that Jesus didn't say, "try" not to worry or "just worry about a few things." No, He actually gave a command, which is not optional – DO NOT WORRY. Webster's Dictionary defines anxiety as: Fear or nervousness about what might happen. Worry is just fear in operation, and as we already learned, it will put a stop to God being able to work in your life. Think about it, Jesus is a gentleman, and if you take your life into your own hands and try to work it out yourself, He isn't going to override you. However, if you surrender control and have a "Jesus Take the Wheel" moment, he will work it out far better than you could have imagined.

Here is the reality – in order for Jesus to take the wheel in your life, you have to let go of it first. Most of us want Jesus in our "car" with us to just direct us where to go, kind of like Siri. The convenient aspect of that thought process is that you still have a choice if you want to go in the given direction or not. When you truly surrender yourself to God, you acknowledge that He knows more about you than you do; therefore, you TRUST Him to take you to the destination for which you were meant. Besides, when you are riding in the passenger seat, you get to enjoy the view. You can sit back and rest - you don't have to maneuver on your own the road and the obstacles that come. Yes, obstacles and storms will still come, but you can stay in the place of peace no matter what comes because of who is in the driver's seat.

This scenario actually occurred in the Bible – except they had a boat instead of a car. Matthew 8:23-26 gives a record of this account. In my paraphrasing, Jesus and His disciples were in a boat when a big storm came up. The disciples were frantic and getting more fearful by the minute as wave after wave covered the boat. However, Jesus was found asleep – not a care in the world! They were upset and woke Him up yelling, "LORD, SAVE US! WE ARE PERISHING!" But Jesus said, "Why are you fearful,

O you of little faith?" He then spoke to the wind and the waves, and the storm calmed down.

Jesus didn't rebuke His disciples because He didn't love them, but He wanted them to recognize that they also have authority and should use it. He was trying to get the point across that if God told you to do something, it doesn't matter what the circumstances look like. He is going to see you through. Not only that, but He has given you authority to speak to any storm that rises against you.

> **If God told you to do it, then He will see you through it.**

I also want to mention that we are to *plan* for tomorrow but not worry about it. There is a big difference between planning - being ready and prepared for what tomorrow brings and worrying about what you can't control. In fact, planning is very important if you struggle with anxiety. The more you can get things out of your head and on paper, the better. Planning helps you to compartmentalize and prioritize your life. Like most of you, I have to balance my life with the many hats I wear. Without properly planning and prioritizing, I can easily end up overwhelmed and anxiety-ridden.

It doesn't have to be just thoughts about the future that brings anxiety. Sometimes we try to cram so much into our day that our minds get cluttered with our to-do lists, appointments, classes, kids' activities, cleaning, and the list goes on.

> **There is a big difference between planning for tomorrow and worrying about what you can't control.**

I am guilty of being a great starter of tasks and then getting distracted. I often start something, go into another room, see something else that needs to be done, and switch my attention to that...then remember something else and start doing that. I end up with my thoughts scattered, and the feeling of anxiety creeping over me. Instead, I have learned (and am still a work in progress) to keep a planner, write down my to-dos and discipline myself to not go to the next task until I am finished with the last one – giving all of my focus to each task one at a time. Having a plan will actually help your anxiety issues. Writing down your to-do's will help you organize your thoughts and alleviate the stress of trying to remember everything in your head. I have become an avid planner user – I rarely leave home without it. This has helped me focus on what I need to focus on: one day at a time – even one task at a time.

BABY STEPS

There is a phrase from the movie, *What About Bob?* that has stayed with me since watching the movie in 1991. Bill Murray's anxiety-ridden character, Bob Wiley, says a phrase over and over to get himself through the day, "baby steps..." He focuses on the little thing that he has to do moment by moment taking "baby steps" through his day. His character suffered from very extreme anxiety about EVERYTHING (Ziskin, Oz, 1991). However, the principle is still a good one. Focus on what is in front of you to do, THIS day. So often when we start thinking about the what-ifs in the future, it gets us anxious because we can't control it. Just focus on the first little thing in front of you. Very soon, you will gain momentum, and just like dominos that are knocked over with a little tap, you will be able to accomplish a lot with very little effort.

BE THANKFUL FOR TODAY

The past and the future are both realities that we have no control over. Living in the past will only keep you trapped to people and circumstances that already happened. In the same regard, living in fear of the future will leave you hopeless. The answer is to live in today. Psalm 118:24 says, *"This is the day the Lord has made; We will rejoice and be glad in it."* Purpose to focus on the day at hand with gratitude or with thankfulness. If you are a "glass half empty"

> Being thankful for the little things opens you up to recognize and receive bigger blessings in your life.

type of person, train yourself to look at the positive in each day. Keep a gratitude journal and record those things you are thankful for each day. Sometimes the things I am thankful for are seemingly insignificant, but being thankful for the little things opens you up to recognize and receive bigger blessings in your life.

For example, as you clean your house, thank God for your home and your belongings that need cleaning. As you are washing your work clothes, thank God for your job. As you are washing your kids' stinky uniforms, thank God that they are well and able to play sports. Do you get my point? Be thankful for the things that we often complain about.

THE POWER OF FORGIVENESS

I mentioned that the past has the power to take you hostage by keeping you trapped with thinking about what has happened to you. The most dangerous trap that we all have fallen into at one time or another is the trap of unforgiveness. Unforgiveness is a deadly poison that you don't want to mess with. It can be something as small as an annoyance or offense to something that was indeed very traumatic. Either way, harboring bitterness in our heart towards someone is more dangerous than you think.

You might have heard the analogy that holding on to unforgiveness is like drinking poison expecting the offender to die. Holding on to hurt has no benefit whatsoever to you. Unfortunately, the thoughts of the wrong done to us play on repeat in our heads, stirring up more anger and hurt in a vicious cycle of pain. Whom do you think presses play on those tormenting thoughts for you? You guessed it, the devil himself. You see, he understands something about unforgiveness that you don't. He knows that the longer you stay bitter, it will spill into all areas of your life. It will not only consume your thoughts but manifest in your body with ulcers and other physical ailments. It will also plague your future relationships with cynicism and distrust. Not to mention that unforgiveness is also a major cause of anxiety.

One of the most sobering consequences of unforgiveness is found in Mark 11:25, "*But when you are praying, first forgive anyone you are holding a grudge against, so that your Father in heaven will forgive your sins, too*" (NIV). God freely forgave us of ALL of our sins. You are forgiven for past sins as well as future sins. The scripture, however, is teaching us that to live fully victorious lives, we need to follow

How many times do we hold the sin of someone else over them – something they can't even make right?

God's example and also forgive others. You don't deserve your forgiveness any more than the person who hurt you deserves his or her forgiveness. Praise God; He forgave us anyway – a debt that was too high for us to pay.

Jesus tells a parable in Matthew 18 about a servant who was brought into the king to pay the debt of ten thousand talents, which he owed. The servant couldn't pay it, so the king was going to sell him and his wife and children to get the money. The servant, however, begged him to have patience with him until he could repay his debt. The king then had compassion on him and actually forgave him of his whole debt. Wow! I think we all could handle that kind of debt cancellation. The parable, however, goes on to say that the same servant had lent only 100 denarii to a fellow servant and went and demanded that the money be paid. When his fellow servant couldn't pay and asked him for more time, he threw him in prison until he could pay it. So, the king hears about what happened and calls him in. Matthew 18:32-34 reads, *"You wicked servant! I forgave you all that debt because you begged me. Should you not also have had compassion on your fellow servant, just as I had pity on you?' And his master was angry, and delivered him to the torturers until he should pay all that was due to him."* Yikes!! This parable, of course, is about our relationship with God. He freely forgave us our sins; yet, how many times do we hold the sin of others over them – something they can't even make right?

Are you holding a debt over someone that he or she will never be able to repay? If so, that means you will be bound to that hurt and that person for the rest of your life. You unknowingly give the devil permission to replay what happened to you over and over and over again. It is like quicksand – the more you struggle with it, the more stuck you get.

Remember when we read about the character of love in chapter one? 1 Cor. 13:5 says, *"It does not dishonor others, it is not self-seeking, it is not easily angered, it keeps no record of wrongs"* (NIV). Love keeps NO RECORD of wrongs. It doesn't say that if the wrong is really bad, you can keep the record. No, it says keep NO record whether it is big or small. Also, remember that God would not tell you to do something that is impossible for you to do. The thing about forgiveness is, it has nothing to do with your feelings. It starts with a *choice* of forgiveness – no matter what the circumstance.

I'm not just telling you to do something that I have never done. I have had to forgive someone for molesting me as a child. Something like that isn't easy to forgive, but it was crucial for being set free. By forgiving that person, I am not saying that what happened to me was okay. What I am doing is empowering myself through forgiveness and taking off the "hand-cuffs" holding me to that circumstance and the pain with it. That unfortunate event in my life doesn't have any control over me – and I REFUSE to let it. I have control over my life and what I allow to affect me. I also will not play the blame game. There is only one person to blame when evil happens and that is the devil!

The devil is also very sneaky at getting us second-hand offended at those who have hurt a loved one or someone close to us. We can be quick to join the bandwagon of offense at school or at work, taking sides with our friends or co-workers. As a mother, I have been surprised at how fast I can get offended by someone who doesn't treat my children right. Wow! The momma bear in me can start growling really fast!

What we need to remember is what Ephesians 6:12 says, *"For we do not wrestle against flesh and blood, but against principalities, against powers, against the rulers of the darkness of this age, against spiritual hosts of wickedness in the heavenly places."* The devil is the author of everything rotten that happens here on the earth. Without his influence, evil would not even exist on the earth. So, I choose to go to the source – the root of the problem and fix the blame where blame is due – the devil. When I do that, I am able to keep no record of wrong done to me from a person.

Imagine every record of wrong you have experienced in your lifetime printed off and put in a box for you to carry everywhere you went. Even on vacation, you had to lug all of those wrongs with you. What a burden! Wouldn't you want to get rid of them as quickly as possible, so you didn't have to drag them around? That heavy load would get in the way of anything and everything you wanted to do. Well, guess what? That is what is happening when you decide to hold onto that wrong done to you. You are weighing yourself down so that you are unable to enjoy life. Do yourself a favor, choose to release yourself from the hurt of the past. Make the decision instead to empower yourself by forgiving and forgetting what lies behind.

Paul reminds us in Philippians 3:13 what we should do with our past, *"forgetting those things which are behind and reaching forward to those things which are ahead…"* Of course, we remember wrongs that were done to us. The difference is if the memory stirs up bitterness and keeps you bound – stuck in that spot or if you use the offense as a stepping stone to climb to higher ground. Satan wants to keep you in the trap of remembering or feeling offended over and over because that will not only hurt you once, but it will hurt you again, and again, and again! Get off of that evil carrousel for good - you will never see any change of scenery if you stay there, getting dizzy with the poison of bitterness.

One way that you can forgive someone is to write it down. Like I said, forgiveness is a choice, not a feeling. Your feelings will never let you move past the hurt. When you write down your forgiveness, it creates a tangible record. It doesn't have to be fancy – just write down whomever it is you forgive and what you forgive them for. Then sign and date it. It is good to do this in a journal so that you can return to it when the old feelings of hurt and offense try to sneak back in (and they will). If and when your feelings try to sabotage your peace, you can turn to your written "forgiveness contract" and remind yourself and the devil (who is known as the accuser) that you did, indeed, forgive so your feelings will have to line up with the facts.

FORGIVE YOURSELF

Maybe you are like Paul, the writer of Philippians, and need to forgive yourself for something. Paul, who formerly was known as Saul, was a Christian killer! He would go from city to city, collecting the Christians to be put to death. He even held the robes of those who stoned Stephen. If he could forgive himself for his evil past, I know you can too! God already forgave you – don't you think it's time to forgive yourself? If you feel that you need to ask someone for forgiveness, then get on with it. Ask God to forgive you first and then the person you wronged, but don't involve someone else if it's going to just stir up strife.

FORGIVE YOUR CIRCUMSTANCES

Forgiving your circumstances is a subject that is not addressed very often but needs to have a light shone on it just the same. Many times, people are put into situations far beyond their control. You might have been born into a very dysfunctional family or even a race of people you feel is oppressed. There is a lot of hatred over situations that happened to the generations before us. Unforgiveness of our ancestor's plight generations ago still has an ugly effect on generations today. When individuals stir up what happened in the past, they attach that hurt to themselves, so it is as if it happened directly to them.

You better believe that Satan is enjoying all of the dissension among the races and people groups. Who do you think has stirred up the riots, the disrespect to authority figures and even to our country? Satan has our society so wrapped up in the past and past hurts that we are blind to what is actually going on.

Harboring anger and bitterness surrounding our government, political parties, and leaders falls into this category as well. You don't have to agree with what is going on, but how you handle it is another subject. If watching the news gets you angry and bitter toward people or groups, don't watch it! The condition of your heart and keeping yourself planted in Christ is far more important than getting a skewed version of the news! Besides, most of what you hear is fear-based anyway. It is a smorgasbord of anxiety for you to feast on. On a side note, God has commanded us to pray for our leaders. He doesn't care if you agree with them or not; your job is to pray (1 Tim. 2:1-3).

ENTER INTO GOD'S REST

Hebrews 4:1-3 says, *"Therefore, since a promise remains of entering His rest, let us fear lest any of you seem to have come short of it. For indeed the gospel was preached to us as well as to them; but the word which they heard did not profit them, not being mixed with faith in those who heard it."* God has promised His people rest. Here we find the answer to why so many of us are not living in that peace. The gospel can only go so far in your life. How far it reaches into your life and the degree in which it can change your life is totally up to you. In return, the same degree that you allow the Word to work in your life is the same degree of rest and peace you will experience. It takes the Word PLUS your faith in that Word to produce the peace and rest you desire.

Living in the Word and having faith in His Word is the place you can experience peace in your life. It doesn't matter who you are or what circumstances you are in; you can live in the peace of God. The key is to DAILY seek Him through prayer and His Word, DAILY check your heart and motives, DAILY take your authority over evil trying to come against you, DAILY forgive. Do you get the point? To stay in the place of peace, you have to make these things a daily habit – a way of life.

CHAPTER 6

REFLECTION QUESTIONS

1. Write down concerns or worries you have about the future.

2. What areas of your life do you have difficulty giving the control over to God? Why?

3. What could you do to help organize your days? Each day write down the three most important things to do for that day only.

4. Make a list of what you are thankful for or keep a gratitude journal each day to remind yourself of your many blessings.

5. Write down whom or what you purpose to forgive. Remind yourself and the devil that forgiveness is a choice, not a feeling.

chapter seven

I DON'T CARE |

When discussing the subject of care, it is best if we identify and define what we are talking about. The first definition of care is how we are to DO something – such as handling a situation or an object carefully. We also define care in regard to maintenance. We are to maintain our vehicles with oil changes and tire rotations. We maintain our homes and clothes by cleaning and repairing them. We care for ourselves by getting check-ups, exercising, and eating right. We are even to maintain relationships that we are in through communication and loving people the way God loves us. Those are all examples of how we should properly care, you could say, be good stewards of what God has given us.

The type of care that I will be referring to, however, is something else entirely. It is what keeps our minds entangled with anxiety. The type of care that I am addressing in this chapter is defined as "suffering of mind." That is exactly what anxiety is – your mind suffering from stress. It is having worry, doubt, and fear overwhelming your soul – all of which you were not created to sustain. When I first started analyzing the cause of my own anxiety, I read that the root of all anxiety is fear. Honestly, I had a hard time with that realization. I didn't think I was afraid of anything. I didn't worry about my children or worry about my needs, so what was the root of my anxiety? I learned, as I have discussed, that you only have faith OR fear in operation at any given time. The two cannot coexist because they are direct opposites of each other and function in the same manner. So, this fear isn't necessarily being afraid of something (although that can be the case at times) but meditating on negative outcomes instead of trusting in God to work it out.

I realized that if my mind wasn't at peace, then the root of fear had to be hidden somewhere. I inspected myself a little further and found that the root of my anxiety was that I cared or was worried about what others thought of me. It didn't matter who I was around; I cared about what everyone thought about what I said or did – good or bad. In truth, I still really struggle with this fear, but it has less power over me every day.

Caring what others think is a real problem. How many times have you felt a prompting to pray for someone but have stopped short because of what people around would think? Too many to count for me – thank you, Lord, for forgiveness and a new day!

The solution for what to do with all of your cares or worries lies in 1 Peter 5:5-9, *"God resists the proud, but gives grace to the humble, Therefore humble yourselves under the mighty hand of God, that He may exalt you in due time, casting all your care upon Him, for He cares for you. Be sober, be vigilant; because your adversary the devil walks about like a roaring lion, seeking whom he may devour. Resist him, steadfast in the faith, knowing that the same sufferings are experienced by your brotherhood in the world."*

PRIDE COMES BEFORE THE FALL

Let's dissect 1 Peter 5:5-9 a little bit. First, it says that God resists the proud but gives grace to the humble. Taking on your own cares and trying to find your own solutions without consulting God first is actually being prideful. Carrying your problems and worries is like telling Jesus, "Thanks for taking care of everything on the cross for me, but I got this." Really? Do you believe Jesus is whom He says He is? Do you believe Isaiah 53:4-5, which says, *"Surely He has borne our griefs and carried our sorrows, Yet we esteemed Him stricken, Smitten by God, and afflicted. But He was wounded for our transgressions, He was bruised for our iniquities; The chastisement for our peace was upon Him, And by His stripes we are healed."* Jesus did it all for YOU! He was harassed, beaten, and tortured, mentally, and physically so that you could have peace.

> **Do you believe Jesus is who He says He is?**

GRACE AND PEACE

The passage in 1 Peter goes on to say that He gives grace to the humble. Grace is having unmerited favor given to you when you didn't do anything to deserve it. In other words, when you trust God enough to give your cares to Him, He does a trade that is very one-sided benefiting you! He takes your problems and cares and gives you favor and ease in its place. I don't know about you, but that sounds like an awesome trade!

Not only does he make a trade with you, but also the grace that He gives is like your EASY button. The office store Staples came out with the 'easy' button as a marketing strategy. They were saying that the products in their store make life easier for you. Well, grace is your easy button! When you give God your cares, you can rest and let Him take care of the mess you were worrying about. And do you know what happens? He takes care of your situation far quicker and easier than you could ever dream possible.

I once had a math professor in college that gave me this type of grace. Math is not my subject, but I really enjoyed this math class because of how this professor taught. I took good notes and would do all of the practices to try to understand the problems. However, another point of anxiety for me was test-taking. It didn't matter how hard I would study; I would totally blank out when I had a test in front of me! I actually had several professors who helped me out at test time because they knew I paid attention in class and understood the material. However, this professor gave me even more favor. When I was the last one sitting in the classroom still working on my test, he came over to me and talked me through each problem that I was having a struggle with. He all but gave me the final answer! I remember the anxiety lifting when he just came and stood beside me with a smile on his face. Jesus does the same thing. He is right next to you every step of the way. All you have to do is cast those cares on Him.

CAST YOUR CARE FOR GOOD

Verse 7 of 1 Peter 5 is where you need to really camp-out and meditate. That means to read the scripture over and over, speaking it out loud and thinking on it until you really get a grasp of what the implications of this verse mean to your life. It says to cast ALL of your care to God - which means to get it away from you and onto Him. All means EVERYTHING – all of it, nothing left over! The word 'cast' means to throw it in a forceful way. You can't be nonchalant about it – you have to get forceful. It will take force because, for some of you, that burden you have been carrying around is heavy. You are going to need some force to cast it on God. Maybe you are saying to yourself, "I'm just not strong enough to do that." Well, then arm yourself with some power and strength from the Word. The Bible says that the JOY of the Lord is your strength. So, be joyful BY FAITH. Get some faith friends or your pastor to come along beside you and help. Remember that God can't get His peace to you until you trade it for your burden. Let me say it as plain as I can - as long as you are carrying your cares (problems), you will continue to struggle with anxiety and panic attacks.

There is another famous scripture in Psalms that people often quote but rarely seem to put into practice. Psalms 46:10 declares, *"Be still, and know that I am God..."* The command to be still literally means to quit trying to do things on your own – just stop! The more you mess with your mess, the worse it is going to get. However, when you take your hands off of it and give it to God, He can work it out for you.

I have counseled a number of children over the years dealing with some heavy situations. One of the things I have had them do is to draw or color their feelings on a piece of paper. I then have the child crumple up that piece of paper and throw it away with force. As an adult, you can do the same thing. Write down your problems or what you are caring about – the areas that cause you the greatest anxiety. Then crumple up that paper and throw it away with force as a physical representation of casting your cares on God.

If you are serious about getting rid of your care for good, get a little grape juice and a cracker and take communion – just you and God (yes,

> **Jesus went to the depths of Hell and paid the price of sin so that you could be absolutely free.**

it is okay), signifying that you are giving God your cares and, in exchange, receiving what Jesus did for you. That is what the cross and communion are all about. His body was broken so that you could be whole. Taking communion is more than a little thing you do at church. It is remembering your covenant with Jesus. It is realizing that Jesus took your anxiety upon

Himself when He was mocked, spit upon, beaten, whipped and nailed to the cross. It didn't stop there, though. Jesus went to the depths of Hell and paid the price of sin so that you could be absolutely free. He would have done it for you if you were the only one on the planet!

After you cast your care to God, I would like to say that that is the end of it. However, Satan will come immediately to check if you are serious. When anxiety comes back, don't get discouraged but keep fighting the good fight of faith. Every time one of those cares or areas of anxiety tries to sneak into your life again, you can declare by faith, "In the name of Jesus, I got rid of that care once and for all and I will not take it back!" Get serious and even mean about it. Don't buckle at the first sign of anxiety trying to come back – because it will. But fight it with the Word of God. Open your Bible to 1 Peter 5:6-8 and read it out loud to yourself, to God and especially to the devil. That is exactly how Jesus fought the devil – by declaring, "IT IS WRITTEN."

HE CARES ABOUT YOU

The second part of verse 7 says, "He cares for you." It is God's job to care for you – to love you. This is the first definition of care that I talked about. It is God's job to provide for you - to keep you in good condition. Jesus provided everything you will ever need to live an abundant life of blessing. However, He isn't going to override your will. If you don't want to receive what Jesus did for you, you don't have to. You don't have to receive healing, health, and prosperity. You can be like a little toddler and say defiantly, "I can do it myself!"

Now if you have had the opportunity to parent a strong-willed child or have been around a toddler at all, you have a little inkling of what God feels like dealing with us! Toddlers don't know what is best for them, they don't look at that cookie and think to themselves, "I understand that the cookie is not good for me, I think that I should eat my green beans instead. I think I will do what is best for me." No, quite the opposite is true – they want what they want NOW regardless if it is good for them or not. In the same manner, when

> Jesus provided everything you will ever need to live an abundant life of blessing.

you are facing anxiety, you have a choice. You can choose the instant gratification and band-aide using alcohol, food, or binge-watching TV, but those things won't make your situation better. In fact, they will most likely make your problems worse. Instead, turn to God. He will show you the best path for your life – trust Him.

YOU HAVE AN ADVERSARY

Let's reread 1 Peter 5:8, *"Be sober, be vigilant; because your adversary the devil walks about like a roaring lion, seeking whom he may devour."* The devil's goal is to destroy you one way or another. He is going around looking for the easy target, just like a hungry lion.

Have you ever watched a nature documentary showing a lion on the prowl for its dinner? She crouches down in the tall grass unbeknownst to her prey. What is she doing? She is taking in the situation, looking and calculating which antelope can be easily plucked from the heard. She doesn't want a big fight, so she looks for one of the babies or injured antelope that won't be able to run as fast. When the lion determines that the time is opportune, she pursues her prey with determination. Most of the time, the antelope is caught of guard and begins running in every direction – every antelope for itself. The lion has to be quick but usually gets her dinner.

The scripture in 1 Peter describes the devil as going after his prey in the same manner. He's looking for easy targets – usually those with weak faith who don't know who they are in Christ and don't know how to fight him off. He comes immediately to take any revelation of the Word that you have received so that you won't know or experience the truth.

Likewise, with the lion, the devil also looks for those found by themselves. There is safety in numbers, people! Go to church, stay hooked up, let your church family know how they can be praying for you. Keep yourself accountable to your Pastors and get involved with serving with your local body of believers.

BE SOBER AND VIGILANT

This is why the scripture tells us to be sober and vigilant. The word, sober, means to be serious. This isn't something to take lightly. We need to be able to recognize the voice of the devil and his schemes when he comes at us with the lies that we have in the past, believed so readily. This is why you need to know who you are in Christ so that when he tells you that you are going to fail, you can wield your Sword of the Spirit and boldly declare – and I mean SHOUT it:

"I OVERCOME YOU DEVIL AND THIS SITUATION BY THE BLOOD OF THE LAMB AND THE WORD OF MY TESTIMONY! (Rev. 12:11) I AM ABOVE AND NOT BENEATH – THE VICTOR, NOT THE VICTIM! (Deut. 28:13) I AM MORE THAN A CONQUEROR THROUGH CHRIST WHO LOVES ME! (Rom. 8:37) ANXIETY DOESN'T BELONG TO ME, I DIDN'T ORDER IT, SO I RETURN IT TO HELL WHERE IT CAME FROM! I RESIST YOU DEVIL IN THE NAME OF JESUS CHRIST, AND THE WORD SAYS THAT WHEN I RESIST YOU, YOU MUST FLEE – SO GOOD-BYE!"

Now, someone might be thinking – "if I say that then the devil will really be after me." He's already looking for whom he can devour, but the Bible says in James 4:7 that if you resist the devil WITH THE WORD, he will flee from you as in terror!

This scenario reminds me of the story of a little bear cub. The bear cub was exploring on his own when he spotted a mountain lion lurking nearby ready to attack. The young bear cub had watched his mom scare off mountain lions before, so the little cub stood up on its hind legs and growled with all its might. He was quite surprised to hear the roar he produced as he watched the lion run off in fear. The little bear cub was impressed with his accomplishment till he turned around and found his mother standing right behind him on her hind legs. It was actually her roar and size that had scared off the lion.

That is the same thing that happens with us. When you come at the devil boldly with the Word in your mouth, He will run in terror because he sees Jesus! He doesn't go fleeing because of you, he goes fleeing because Christ already whooped him, and when you come in the Name of Jesus, it's just as if Jesus Himself is standing in front of him saying it!

Being care/anxiety-free can be a reality in your life. I encourage you to cast your cares daily onto God. Let Him take your mess and make it a message. Let Him take your test and make it your testimony. Let Him work a miracle in your life and situation today.

CHAPTER 7

REFLECTION QUESTIONS

1. Write down what you feel the root of your anxiety is. In other words, what triggers you to feel anxious?

2. Write a letter to Jesus, acknowledging what He did on the cross for you. Thank Him for your healing and for the favor He gives you through grace.

3. Cast your care on Him. You may want to write each care on separate pieces of paper or all on one sheet. Don't worry about being neat. You may want to make a list or use a combination of drawing and writing. Next, crumble the paper(s) up and cast it (throw) it away forcefully.

4. Take communion as a tangible remembrance of this great exchange. You can go to the link provided, and I will lead you in a time of communion.

5. Rewrite the declaration I gave and post it somewhere you will see it regularly. Speak it or even yell it when anxiety tries to come back on you!

chapter eight

BE VIGILANT |

There are so many aspects of being vigilant over your life that it required a chapter all its own. To be vigilant means to be on the lookout – to be aware of your surroundings. Spiritually speaking, you are to pay attention to outside sources and situations that put you in a position to fall into the devil's traps. In other words, you are to pay attention to seemingly innocent day in and day out scenarios that have the potential of stealing the progress you have made spiritually.

The devil uses what he has at his disposal in the physical realm to get the upper hand in your life, and he is very sneaky in doing so. Because he has dominion on the earth, he uses earthly, everyday situations to knock you off your course. Remember, he doesn't play fair. Now, we don't have to be scared of him, but we do need to have wisdom on how we unknowingly open ourselves up for attacks. The following areas are access points that the devil will use to pull you away from the Word and cause the spiritual seed in your life to not reach maturity.

BUSYNESS

Being too busy is an area that has caught all of us in its trap. It seems that there are more and more activities that suck every free moment that we have dry. I especially dread the months of December and May for how insanely busy life gets. My calendar's white space is few and far between, especially during those months. Like I said, being too busy was one of the major reasons why anxiety snuck up on me so severely. My time and attention divided into too many directions caught up to me in a hurry.

I believe that one of the devil's greatest strategies and weapons used against us is keeping us busy. Think about it: How many times have you missed church due to another scheduled event, or you purposefully plan a little R&R on the weekend? Don't get me wrong, a little R&R is needful, but not at the cost of letting your spiritual life falter. True rejuvenation comes from spending time with God because that is what we were created to do.

The number one reason people find themselves needing spiritual counseling is that they have neglected to feed their spirits properly. The Bible even warns against this tactic used by the devil in Mark 4:18-19, *"Now these are the ones sown among thorns; they are the ones who hear the word, and the cares of this world, the deceitfulness of riches, and the desires for other things entering in choke the word, and it becomes unfruitful."* What this means is that even if you hear the Word being preached here or there and read your Bible now and again, those good intentions are choked out by the other 'stuff' in your life.

Jesus says in Matthew 16:25-26, *"For whoever desires to save his life will lose it, but whoever loses his life for My sake will find it. For what profit is it to a man if he gains the whole world, and loses his own soul? Or what will a man give in exchange for his soul?"* In other words, if you spend time filling your life with busy schedules, what will you gain in the end? Is it worth it?

Purpose to start every day with God in prayer and reading your Bible. When you give the first part of your day to God with the Word and prayer and the first part of your week to God in church, everything else will fall into place. Your soul will find rest from the busyness of life.

WHAT ARE YOU WATCHING?

What are you spending your time watching? My husband once went to see a woman who had asked for prayer for depression. When he stepped into her home, he was first met with darkness – every window was covered to keep any light out. Clutter and filth met him everywhere he looked – he couldn't even find a place to sit, nor did he want to. As he looked around, he saw a big pile of scary

> **What you see, hear, taste, smell, and touch are all gateways to your soul.**

movies sitting by the TV. He asked if she watched them a lot, and she confirmed that she did because she liked the thrill of being scared. Well, my husband knew right then that no amount of prayer was going to help this woman. She was inviting fear and depression right in by watching that stuff and creating an atmosphere for depression. Therefore, any prayer that my husband could have prayed for her would have been voided by what she was opening herself up to. If this describes you (feeding on "thrillers"), stop at once! Watching fear-based 'entertainment' gives a big open door for the devil to waltz right in and create his own entertainment with your life. You are not to give a place to the devil (Eph. 4:27), and watching fear and death-based entertainment gives a big place for him to sit right down on the couch and get cozy with you.

You may think that what you watch is no big deal, and that is exactly what the enemy wants you to think. However, he knows that what you see, hear, taste, smell, and touch are all gateways to your soul – the area that he wants to wreak havoc with.

Books fall into this same category as what you watch. In fact, I think books can sometimes be worse because they can create such vivid imagery in your mind. Sorry to tell you women, but smutty romance novels are really just soft porn. I have read some romance novels that would have been really good, but then they threw in a very graphic sex scene with more detail than a rated R movie would be allowed to show. Just because it is in a book form doesn't make it okay to consume. When picking out your entertainment, ask God for direction and discernment. He will help you make healthy choices for your soul.

WHAT DO YOU LISTEN TO?

Another area that you have to keep vigilant in is what you listen to. Most people think that the music they listen to has no effect on them. The truth of the matter is that music is tightly connected to your soul. People listen to music to feel a connection to it. As a music teacher and a performer, I have experienced firsthand the emotions that one song can bring out of individuals as well as myself. I have felt connected to the lyrics and the music as well as to the individuals that I am performing with.

God created music not just for our entertainment, but He created it because it is an amazing way to connect to Him. The scripture tells us that God inhabits the praises of His people. That means that He connects with you when you worship Him in a deeper way. Well, if music can connect you to God and others, it sure as well can connect you to the devil. When you listen to songs filled with hate, death, destruction, sex, lying, cheating, and foul language, again, it opens an opportunity for you to be connected to those things.

Music gets down in your soul like nothing else. When teaching my teenagers about this concept, I had them listen to a secular song – nothing bad, just a regular song that you would hear on the radio. I had them really pay attention to how the song made them feel, what the lyrics were saying and how their spirits felt. After that, we listened to a worship song. I had them note the difference in how they felt. They noticed how the worship music immediately brought a peace to their soul. Did I make them not listen to secular music again? Of course not, there is a lot of good music out there that is just fun to listen to, but I wanted them to understand the power that music has and to use discretion with what they allow themselves to listen to.

Often athletes listen to music to get ready for a game – why? Because the music has an effect on them – gets them in the right frame of mind. Well, if music can help you get in the right frame of mind, it is also possible for it to get you into the wrong frame of mind. The devil knows how powerful music is because he was the chief musician in heaven before he rebelled against God. Again, he does not play fair – if he can get you to open a door to him through what you listen to (just because it has a good beat), he will.

On a side note - if you are wrestling with anxiety or depression, turn on some praise and worship music and you will immediately start to feel it lift. The devil can't stand in the presence of God, which is exactly what worship does - it brings God's presence on the scene. Therefore, worship music is a sure way to get rid of the devil in a hurry and get you into a place of peace.

WHAT ARE YOU EATING AND DRINKING?

Food has such an enormous impact on us physically and mentally. Many times (probably more often than not), we use food for pleasure. It comforts us and makes us feel better. Just as music is referred to as *soul* music, we also have *soul* food. Just the mention of soul food gets our mouths watering. It's often the food that we grew up with – food that brings back memories and has a special place in our traditions and cultures.

Although food, as well as music, movies, books, and other forms of entertainment, is a good thing and a needful thing, it can also be a two-edged sword. We can't live without food; therefore, the temptation to abuse our bodies with unhealthy food or to consume unhealthy amounts of food (too much or too little) is ever-present.

What you eat or drink has an impact on your mental health just as much as your physical health, which is why the devil uses it. For example, we now have science and research that reveals how detrimental sugar is to us physically and mentally. We know the negative ramifications of smoking, drinking, and consuming other detrimental items. However, most of us have struggled with an addiction at some level to sugar, caffeine, alcohol, nicotine, or other drugs. Addiction is simply your body dictating to you what it thinks it needs instead of your spirit (the real you) dictating to your body what it actually needs.

My husband likes to drink a pop every afternoon. However, as a practice, he denies himself a pop if his body starts screaming to him that he NEEDS one. He is living a fasted life. That just means that he keeps his body in check. He will fast (or deny himself) something if he feels he has an addiction to it.

I know that this area is a real battle for so many people. I can tell you right now that if you are trying to gain control of an addiction by your own will power, you might have some success, but that success will usually be short-lived. Just compare the attendance of gyms in January versus a month later, and you will find a drastic difference. The reason that your will power doesn't get the job done is that the root of the problem goes deeper than your will power has strength for. You need to build little habits into your life that will act as scaffolding around the life changes you are in search of. Use your will power to build the habits and your habits will build the life you want.

Years ago, I was starting to have some digestive problems, and so I sought God on the issue. I felt that he was telling me to stay away from dairy as well as oily or greasy things. So, I also sought after the expertise of a dietician about what was going on, and she confirmed what I believed God was telling me. The reason these things were giving me problems was because I don't have a gall bladder. Well, I had a choice and still have a choice every day with whether or not I am going to adhere to what I now know will help me feel better or go ahead and eat what my flesh desires and reap the consequences later. You are a result of what you allow into yourself through what you see, hear, and eat.

WHO ARE YOU SPENDING TIME WITH?

The last place that you are to be vigilant is in relationships. Relationships are an important area to be watchful of because, like I stated before, you will start to act like and sound like who you are around the most.

I'm sure you have heard of the circle of influence. Your circle of influence is the people whom you keep closest to you. They are your best friends, the ones who know your deepest secrets. They are the ones whom you spend most of your time with. These people have great influence on what you think, how you act, even what you wear.

This phenomenon is very noticeable in middle school-aged students (whom I teach). In any middle school, on any given day, you will see little pods of girls dressed, standing, and talking exactly the same. It is a little comical to watch; however, we as adults do the same thing – only with higher stakes.

The people you spend the most time with will influence how you think about situations and how you respond to those situations. For example, say you had someone who was rude to you or said something hurtful to you. Well, you tell your squad all about it, and now they are riled up and giving you "advice" on what you should do (none of which is probably godly). You

> You will never rise higher than your circle of influence.

will never rise higher than your circle of influence. That is an important statement that you need to read again.

Sometimes the best action you can take to change your life is to rearrange your circle of influence. You don't have to cut ties with your friends, but you need to find people who will elevate you. You need to surround yourself with individuals who will pray with you and maybe share some scriptures with you when you are going through a rough time. Find someone who will fill you up instead of feed the flame of bitterness. Some of you are thinking, "do those people really exist?" Yes, they do. You just have to look in the right places (and the bar isn't it).

I have a Bible study group that does just that. If one of us is dealing with an issue, we don't get caught up in reliving the details, gossiping about it, or talking about how bad it is. We share scripture with each other and pray for each other and give godly advice on how to deal with it. Those are the type of people you need to surround yourself with. Like I said, you don't get rid of your friends, but you should be very selective with whom you are allowing to speak into your life. The devil definitely uses relationships to lead you off the biggest cliff he can find. You may not jump off a bridge if your friends told you too, but you might follow some advice that could cause big problems.

If you are struggling to find those who could influence you in a positive way – go to church! We also live in this awesome age of technology. You can listen to uplifting messages from awesome ministers that will influence you in the right way. Again, whoever you listen to the most is whom you will emulate the most. I don't know about you, but I want to surround myself with positive, faith-talking people who build me up and help me out of my ruts, not pull me down.

THAT SPECIAL SOMEONE

Another very important aspect of relationships is whom you date and especially marry. Why discuss this in a book about anxiety? Because whomever you allow in your life will either help or hinder you. The person you open yourself intimately to WILL affect every single area of your life. This person is whom you let into your very innermost circle of influence because you are joined to him or her spirit, soul, and body. I don't care what society says; once you are physically intimate with someone, you will be soul connected to that person. This is not something to treat lightly.

You need to get ahold of the truth of how precious you are. You are worthy of being treated with dignity, respect, and honor. I once dated a guy whom I thought was really nice and kind. One day I needed to go to a town about 45 minutes away for a hair appointment and some other errands. I was scheduled to work, performing in a tourist music show that evening, so he wanted to spend some time with me beforehand. He told me that he would drive me up in his convertible, which I thought was really sweet. Well, as I got my hair done, he sat there moping and disgruntled because he had to wait. He then was perturbed to help me run my other errands because it cut into what he wanted to do. To top it off, he got upset that I didn't want the top down in the convertible for the drive home because I didn't want to mess up my hair. his attitude that day, you may say, was nothing big; however, his little pouty attitude from not getting his way was a HUGE red flag for me. The undertone of his attitude was selfish. He didn't really care about me. He only cared about his agenda and how I was affecting him.

This is what I want you to hear – I refused to settle with just anyone. I had high expectations and standards that were not only my standards but were God's standards for His daughter. I wasn't going to settle for anyone who wouldn't love me just as Christ loved the church. Side note – you should be dating for marriage. Don't spend your time with someone you know you don't want to marry – and you definitely shouldn't waste your time with someone who doesn't love God and have a personal relationship with Him.

My husband treats me like the princess that God says I am. He puts my wants and wishes above his. He values me and my gifts and talents. He makes me feel like the most important person in His life next to God – and I know I am. He would tell you that I am his hobby! That means that he is interested in me and wants to spend his time and money on me! Now, that is a catch!

If you are not married yet, do not settle with just anyone. Be vigilant with whom you give your heart to. He/she better treat you with the utmost respect and love. That person should also love God above everything else – not just giving lip service, but his or her actions should say that they love God as well.

I could write a whole book on the subject of relationships because it is so vitally important to your life – spirit, soul, and body. However, here are some questions to get you started on what to look for in someone to date and marry:

- ✓ Does he/she love God? Not just with lip service but attend and serve in church.
- ✓ Is he/she respectful to authority figures? For example; with his/her parents, teachers, boss, and law officers.
- ✓ Does he/she have any addictive bad habits that you know of?
- ✓ Is he/she a procrastinator or prompt to do tasks?
- ✓ How are his/her relationships with their family members? If estranged, why?

The bottom line is that you understand and accept that you are precious and valuable. If you truly want to be in health and prosper just as your soul prospers as 3 John 2 says, then you are going to have to stand guard over your life. Take some time to examine each of these areas. Be honest with yourself, making note of changes that need to be made. Change is hard at first, but it is so important if you are serious about seeing real, positive results in your life.

CHAPTER 8

REFLECTION QUESTIONS

1. How has the busyness of life affected you physically, mentally, and spiritually?

2. Have you ever considered that what you watch or listen to directly affects your soul? Take time to examine what you regularly watch or read. Have you grown calloused to imagery and subjects that are not becoming for a child of God to be entertained by?

3. Go through your playlist. Ask God for direction on what music you might need to alleviate. For example, if you struggle with depression, you probably shouldn't listen to music that makes you feel sad.

4. Do you struggle with an addiction of any kind? Write down anything you feel in bondage to. Just as you did with your cares, cast any addiction over to Jesus. Ask Him for wisdom and guidance on what natural steps you need to take to gain complete healing and freedom.

5. Think about each person in your circle of influence. Does he/she help or hinder positive change in your life? Do you need to make any changes to your circle of influence to experience positive change and growth?

chapter nine

THE SECRET PLACE |

What if I told there was a secret place that you could go where you would be safe and secure at all times? What if I told you it was a place of overwhelming peace and rest? It is also a place you could go to gain wisdom and understanding for problems in your life that need answers. I'm guessing you would want to know where this wonderful place is and how to get there. Yes, this place really does exist. It is a place that I not only visit but that I strive to live in.

How can that be? As we learned, you are a spirit; you live in a body and have a soul. The spirit realm and the physical realm actually co-exist together. Many situations that we come up against in the physical realm are actually a direct result of what is happening in the spiritual realm. Ephesians 6:12 says, *"For we are not fighting against flesh-and-blood enemies, but against evil rulers and authorities of the unseen world, against mighty powers in this dark world, and against evil spirits in the heavenly places"* (NLT).

We also learned that we use faith to bring the things we cannot see from the supernatural into the natural. Therefore, we can live or abide in the secret place by faith. We have access to a vault of treasure that far exceeds that of material wealth.

The secret place is not just to visit, but we are to dwell – to live there. Psalm 91 begins by saying, *"He who dwells in the secret place of the Most High shall abide under the shadow of the Almighty."*

If you want to be in that secret place, it says that you must abide under the shadow. Now, if you are in the shadow of someone, you are in very close proximity to that person. Better yet, if you are living and dwelling in the shadow, then you are never separated from that person. Wow! Just think how much you would know about someone if you never left his or her side? I think of conjoined twins who obviously spend every waking and sleeping moment together. They are inseparable from each other. Therefore, they are able to do everyday tasks together and even finish one another's sentences without skipping a beat.

> The secret place is not just to visit, but we are to dwell – to live there.

We are to be so connected to our heavenly Father that living with Him is all we know. Jesus said that everything He did was what the Father told Him to do, and everything He said was what He heard the Father say. We can have the same relationship with our Heavenly Father that Jesus had. Remember, Jesus walked this earth just like you and me – a human. He got tired like we get tired. He felt pain and sorrow like we feel pain. However, if you read the gospels, you will find that He lived differently than we live. He lived fully connected to the Father. He had His ear to Him at all times.

Abiding in the shadow of the Almighty does more for us than just keep us in close proximity to God. Verse 2 goes on to declare, *"He is my refuge and my fortress."* Notice that this is personal – He is MY refuge and MY fortress. He cares about YOU and taking care of YOU. The Word refuge means: A shelter or a place of protection and trust; it is a shelter from the storm. This isn't just a flimsy shelter. The word says that He is my FORTRESS. A fortress is built for the purpose of protecting and defending from attacks. How awesome is that? God is your defender and His defense is the only defense you need.

The rest of Psalm 91 lists one way after another of how God is protecting you from the evil one. It even tells you in verse 11, *"He shall give His angels charge over you, to keep you in all your ways."* You have angels assigned to you to help and protect you and to give you the advantage in situations you face. The enemy doesn't play fair and neither should you! But you can't do it on your own – it is vital that you stay and keep yourself in close relationship with God. Where He tells you to go, you go. What He tells you to say, you say.

I love the end of Psalm 91, starting in verse 14. This is God's promise to **YOU** and what happens when you choose to abide in Him. He says,

"Because he has set his love upon Me, therefore I will deliver him; I will set him on high because he has known My name. He shall call upon Me, and I will answer him; I will be with him in trouble; I will deliver him and honor him. With long life, I will satisfy him and show him My salvation." How cool is that? That is God's promise to you and He keeps His promises.

HAVE EARS TO HEAR

Jesus had ears to hear what God was speaking to Him, and He encourages us to do the same. In Mark 4:23, Jesus says, *"If anyone has ears to hear, let him hear."* Notice that He said IF ANYONE. "IF" means that you have a choice to hear Him or not. The scripture tells us that He speaks to us in a still small voice. That means you have to get quiet – push back the noise around you to hear what He is saying.

I have a little student who will come up to me during class to ask for something. Now, I teach music and, as you can imagine it can get quite loud in the classroom. Well, this little girl seems to pick the loudest times to ask me a question. She doesn't just pick the loudest time, but she also speaks in a voice a little louder than a whisper. I can see her lips moving but can't hear a single thing coming out of her mouth. I have to bend down and put my ear right up to her mouth to be able to hear what she is saying to me. She requires my full attention if I want to hear and understand her. I have to block out the noise around me and focus on her.

That is what we need to do with God. At times the circumstances around us and even our own emotions can get loud. They can distract us from hearing from God. God isn't going to get louder just because your surroundings are loud. No, you are going to have to adjust and incline your ear to Him. You have to lean in and listen to what He is speaking to you – and He IS speaking.

> How big or small you make God in your life is how big or small He will be in your life.

I recently was meditating on this scripture, and the Lord dropped something in my heart that I immediately wrote down. He said, "How big or small you make Me in your life is how big or small I will be in your life." Reread that and let it soak in. How much emphasis are you giving the Word in your life? For example: Are you listening to God throughout your day – keeping a running dialog with him about everything you encounter? Or do you have your devotional time every day, but then go about your activities solo? Do you see God as a box that you check off each week on Sunday? Or do you wake up on Sunday mornings and think to yourself that you went to church this month already, so you're good? Maybe you have let yourself drift so far away that the thought of coming back to Him scares you.

If the last example is you, don't be afraid to turn back to God. The story of the prodigal son in the Bible was put there to show us God's reaction when His son or daughter comes back home. He puts His arms around you and celebrates your return. No condemnation!

Again, how big or small you make God in your life is how big or small He will be in your life. As a pastor, many times, we are called to pray for someone in a crisis situation. It is much easier to pray with someone who has had a consistent relationship with God than with someone who only seeks God out in an emergency. Don't get me wrong; I'm glad for those who call when they are in a crisis emergency situation – they are turning in the right direction, and I am thankful for the opportunity to minister into their lives. However, much of the time, those situations could have been avoided if they had stayed in close fellowship with God in the first place. Even as a pastor, I will find myself in unfavorable situations because I let my spiritual guard down. It happens to all of us.

God's desire is to be so much more than an emergency back-up plan in your life. He wants to be involved in every aspect – helping you, guiding you, healing you, giving you wisdom, helping you walk in love, helping you stay in peace. The thing is, He isn't going to force himself on you. You get to decide how much of your life you want to give Him access to. It is up to you and you alone to determine how involved you want God to be in your life.

Think about the headaches you could have saved yourself if you listened to God and simply did or said what He wanted you to do or say. Our flesh would like to tell us that following Christ so closely would be a terrible life and that we would never have fun again. Contrarily, it says in Jeremiah 29:11 that He only has good plans for you. Those plans include prospering you and having fun along the way. Remember: He is the one who invented "fun" in the first place. Satan has been trying to replicate what God created from the beginning. He can't create anything new – he just twists what God has already made.

ABIDE IN THE VINE

Jesus says in John 15:5, *"I am the vine, you are the branches. He who abides in Me, and I in him, bears much fruit; for without Me you can do nothing."* Through this scripture, Jesus paints us a picture of what our relationship with Him should look like and be like if we want fruitful (successful) lives.

The branches obviously are the part of a tree that produces fruit. I have never seen apples grow straight from the trunk of a tree. Yet, many people and even Christians believe that if God wants to do something, He can just do it with or without us. That is not true at all. We are to be His hands and feet on this earth. He is the vine – the vine has an important job of bringing everything that the branches need to produce the fruit. The branches never worry that the supply of water and nutrients won't be there. They take in whatever is supplied to them and then in the right season they produce.

Just as God needs us to produce good spiritual fruit in this world, we need Him to be our supply. A limb that has been broken off of the tree might look good for a couple of days, but slowly the leaves will lose color and the branches will become dry. The branch cannot sustain life on its own, separate from the tree. You might find short-term success doing things your own way, but sooner or later, the success that you are trying to produce on your own will be dried up like that tree branch.

It is prideful to think you can do things on your own or in your way. Yet, the idea of being independently successful is glamourized. Frank Sinatra even sang about, "I did it my way." Well, sorry to break it to you, Frank, but you should not want to do things "your way." We are designed to need each other and most importantly, to need God.

Notice in John 15:5, it says that you can DO NOTHING without Him. Why do you think there are so many celebrities or people who seem to have every earthly possession to make them happy yet suffer from depression or die by suicide? They are putting pressure on themselves to be successful in and of themselves instead of being connected to the life source – Jesus. Living independently from God might not manifest as depression, but it will manifest. Anger, frustration, disappointment, loneliness, bitterness, hate, arrogance, meanness, being just plain miserable are all "fruit" that will produce in your life when you try to do things your own way.

Did you know that your desires for your life were actually put there by God? God gave you your desires. He put your talents and interests into your DNA. He knows what you will be most fulfilled doing. He gave you your personality and your likes and dislikes. He wants more than anything to bless you with your deepest dreams and desires. He will give you great success without stress and sorrow and frustration attached. You can live the life God intended for you while having fun and being joyful and peaceful.

PLANTED BY THE RIVERS

Psalm 1 says, *"Blessed (Happy, fortunate, prosperous, and enviable) is the man who walks and lives not in the counsel of the ungodly [following their advice, their plans and purposes], nor stands [submissive and inactive] in the path where sinners walk, nor sits down [to relax and rest] where the scornful [and the mockers] gather. But his delight and desire are in the law of the Lord, and on His law (the precepts, the instructions, the teachings of God) he habitually meditates (ponders and studies) by day and by night. And he shall be like a tree firmly planted [and tended] by the streams of water, ready to bring forth its fruit in its season; its leaf also shall not fade or wither; and everything he does shall prosper [and come to maturity]"* (AMPC).

Basically, this scripture is saying that you are going to be BLESSED when you stay planted and fed by the Word of God. A tree planted next to a river never lacks what it needs. In fact, did you notice that it said, "He shall be like a tree firmly planted by the STREAMS?" Meaning there is more than one stream. As I was studying this out, the Lord took me back to Genesis and the Garden of Eden. There is a specific tree that we are supposed to be like, and that is the tree of life, which is the representation of abundant life.

The tree of life and the tree of the knowledge of good and evil were both in the garden. Genesis 2:10 reads, *"Now a river went out of Eden to water the garden, and from there it parted and became four riverheads."* So, being planted by the streams or rivers refers to your life being like the tree of life. You are to continually feed on the Word of God, for it contains everything you need.

When God created the Garden of Eden, He gave man the job of tending it. As Adam cared for the land, God provided the increase. What this means for you is that you have the job of tending the "soil" or your life. You are to make sure that you keep the weeds from growing in around the Word and choking it out. When you stay planted in the Word, you will be like Adam and Eve and be taken care of without having to worry about a thing. The only concern you should have is staying connected to the Word of God. When you stay connected, you will dwell in that secret place of the Most High.

CHAPTER 9

REFLECTION QUESTIONS

1. What does it mean to you to have God as your refuge and fortress?

2. Read Psalm 91:14. How does this promise from God make you feel? Do you believe that He will perform His Word for you? If you don't feel like that promise can be a reality in your life, why do you feel that way?

3. How big or small have you made God in your life? What areas do you need to give Him more access to?

4. What desires or dreams do you have? List some of your talents – big and small. Spend time talking to God about the plans He has for you.

5. Write down some ways in which you can tend the garden of your life and cultivate good soil.

chapter ten

MAINTENANCE |

The keyword in this chapter is maintenance. Have you noticed that you have to work to maintain almost everything around you? Your house, car, appliances, and nearly everything you own has to have proper maintenance. You can't expect to buy a car and never change the oil or the tires or even put gas in it but still expect it to last very long for you. If you get a new car but refuse to maintain it, it isn't the car's fault when it quits working. The same is true for your life. God can change your circumstances and heal you spirit, soul, and body, but you have a part to play in the maintenance of your life.

The point about maintenance is that it is an ongoing, everyday task. The devil isn't going to take a day off, so you can't take a day off either. Remember, God sent Jesus to give you the victory in and over your circumstances. Jesus already won – you just have to maintain that walk of victory in your life through diligence. The fact of the matter is, even if the devil isn't directly messing with you, we live in a fallen world that is in a constant state of decay and, therefore, needs constant upkeep. I wish that I only had to do one good workout to be physically fit, but that just isn't the case. The older I get, the less time I can take between workouts before my body is telling me about it. However, if we daily give attention to some practical things in small ways, we will be better off.

> **Jesus already won your victory; you just have to maintain it in your life through diligence.**

I read a book by Teri Savelle Foy entitled, *5 Things Successful People Do*

Before 8 A.M. I recommend reading this book for more insight on how to set yourself up for success. In the book, Teri talks about how successful people have one thing in common: They take time to invest in themselves. Now the habits that people do to invest in themselves vary to some degree, but the one thing they have in common is that they get up early and give attention to their spirit, soul, and body before anything else.

When I decided to get serious about putting anxiety and stress out of my life, I started getting up early to invest in myself before my day dictated my time. I challenged myself to spend more time with God, to exercise regularly, and start other healthy habits that would help me maintain a stress-free life. Again, I recommend Teri's book for more helpful ideas to include, but I will share with you in this section the habits that I have created to maintain a calm and peaceful soul.

Some of the habits I do daily should be non-negotiable in your life as well – such as spending time with God. However, the amount of time and when you choose to spend your quality time with God will be different for everyone. I will say that there is something very empowering with spending the first part of your day with Him. It sets your focus right and helps you to renew your mind each day. It also seems that everything else in the day runs so much smoother when you give your attention to God first.

JUST FOR TODAY

Like I said, maintenance is an everyday thing. Maintaining a healthy life - spirit, soul, and body is about the little habits you build into your daily routines to help scaffold a changed life. It takes 21 days to develop a habit. Therefore, as you are trying to make changes in your life, don't give up. Be like Paul in Philippians 3:14 and "press toward the goal."

The most precious thing you have in your possession is the 24 hours in front of you. So, take your new habit one day at a time. Treat every day as the first day of your new habits. Have you ever noticed that it's easy to start something new? However, the newness wears off quickly, and eventually we quit the new habit. Treat every day as the first day of the rest of your life.

I adopted this concept of being able to do anything for one day from a Dale Carnegie workshop I attended. The poem on a bookmark I received, written by Sibyl F. Partridge, discusses daily habits that will make a huge impact in your life. It is all about making choices every day. It starts by stating:

Just for today I will be happy…

Just for today I will try to adjust myself to what is, and not try to adjust everything to my own desires…

Just for today I will take care of my body…
Just for today I will strengthen my mind…

The poem goes on to list things that most people want in their lives but lack the discipline to continue them day in and day out. As the poem suggests, success comes from making habit forming choices daily.

It simply comes down to a choice to take back control of your life. Again, if you want to see changes, then you will have to make changes. Don't just hope or wish that your life will be better, but take control of what you are able to control right now and let God take care of the rest. The following list is what I do to help "tend" and cultivate my life for God to work in. They are practical things that I do each day to keep anxiety at bay and stay *planted* in Him.

5 IMPORTANT HABITS TO START

1. Make a Plan

I used to think that writing my weekly and daily agenda down was a waste of time. I thought that I could keep my schedule and to-do's straight in my mind; besides, I didn't want to become rigid with my time.

Now, I will say that when I had young children at home, I would get frustrated when I tried to have a schedule that never panned out. I have since learned that just because I write down a plan, doesn't mean that I have to stick with it, nor does it mean that if I waver from my original plans, I failed!

I really felt that I had failed if I didn't keep up with my unrealistic schedule and to-do list – remember "Wonder Poppins?" Instead of using a plan as a tool to help me, it was a source of anxiety. I didn't know how to properly plan my days to fit the season of life I was in. So, I went from one extreme of trying to have every minute planned with a 4-year old, 2-year old, and infant (INSANE) to deciding to do the extreme opposite and not have any plan! Oh, boy! That 26-year old momma of three needed help!

We have seasons and times in our lives that require different kinds of planning. There are times that it is necessary and vital to have a rigid schedule for our days and other times when we need to be flexible. How do you know what type of plan is best for you? Ask your creator! Ask Him to show you what you need to do for your time of life and your personality.

There are so many different kinds of planners and systems out there to choose from. It may take a short while to find what works best for you. I have found for myself that I am very visual. If I write something down, I may not have to even look at it again because I will most likely remember it. Therefore, digital planners don't work very well for me because they don't allow me to write it in physically. I also find great satisfaction in checking items off of a to-do list. I admit that I will even write down a task after I have done it just for the satisfaction of checking it off! Therefore, I know that I need a planner that allows me to write lists and check them off. I am also all about being creative, so the planners that come with pretty stickers are perfect for me! I know it seems silly, but when something is pretty, I will look at it more – including a planner.

The reason that using a planner is so important when it comes to maintaining a life of peace is that it de-clutters your mind. When I write down my schedule, I often find that the list of to-do's in my mind is really not as daunting as I have made them out to be. I don't know about you, but when I don't write something down, I go over it in my mind so that I don't forget it. I will think of what I still need to do while doing something else. That isn't the kind of multi-tasking that you should do! By writing my to-do list down, I am able to concentrate solely on one task at a time – giving full attention to that one thing.

2. Read the Word

Praying and reading the Bible is so fundamental to a believer's life, but so many people are failing to practice the basics. If you watch professional sports, you are watching people be the best at the basics in their sport. If you want to see real change in your life, then get really good and faithful with practicing the basics: Praying and reading the Bible. However, most of us prioritize reading Facebook before reading the Good Book or reading the news before reading the Good News!

There are many different plans out there to follow. Maybe you like to use a daily devotional, or maybe you like to follow a reading plan. Either way, get your daily dose of the Word before anything else.

When you sit down to read the Bible, ask God to speak to you through His Word and thank Him for revelation of what you read. For a more meaningful time in the Word, after reading a chapter, take a verse that spoke to you and really think (meditate) on it. Write that verse in a journal accompanied with how you feel the Holy Spirit is speaking to you through it. End by including a little one-sentence prayer of applying that verse in your life.

Jesus refers to the Word as the Bread of Life. It is our spiritual food that we need to eat daily for our spirits to stay strong. Like we previously discussed, it also will build your faith since faith comes by hearing the Word. Make reading the Bible THE number one priority each day.

3. Prayer Time

Prayer connects you to your power source – it is what will keep you going, no matter what your day throws at you.

It is amazing to me that we will make sure that our phones are charged before even making sure we are charged. We even keep a charger with us just in case we need to recharge during the day. Why? Because like it or not, our lives are tied to our phones. How much more should we be connecting our spirits to our power source (God) through prayer – each day and throughout the day? When you feel a little low, pray and get powered back up.

Don't get caught up with how much time is sufficient for prayer. I have found that the more time I spend in quality prayer, the more time I *want* to spend in prayer. My designated prayer time in the morning is invaluable to me. This is when I don't have any other distractions vying for my attention. I have my daily appointment with God that I am unwilling to miss out on. Don't try to be too rigid with this precious time with your Father. Allow the Holy Spirit to guide your prayer time. In fact, sometimes just sitting in His presence, not saying a single word but listening for Him to speak is what is needed most.

Although I have quality prayer time with God in the morning, I don't leave Him there in my living room - I take God with me all day. I thank Him as I'm cleaning. I talk to Him as I'm working. I ask for wisdom on how to handle different situations or creativity with whatever I am doing. I purpose to have a running conversation with Him all day long.

I spend time praying in the spirit (praying in tongues) to edify myself, which also helps me to hear from heaven. God has given us such a wonderful gift to be able to pray in the Holy Spirit. I realize that many of you reading this book may not believe in praying in tongues or that it is even for Christians to use today. Well, you're too late to tell me that it isn't for me. There have been countless times in my life when praying in the spirit has been crucial.

The Bible explains it in this way: That when we don't know how or what to pray, the Holy Spirit intercedes for us (Romans 8:26-27). We only have so much natural knowledge. Do you really think that you know how to best pray for every given situation? That is why the Holy Spirit is also known as the Helper. We desperately need Him and His help, especially when it comes to prayer.

Praying in the spirit is like using a spiritual power tool. Say you want to cut down a tree but only have a hand saw to get the job done. Eventually, you will fall the tree, but it won't be without a lot of time and effort from you. However, if you use a power-saw on that same tree, it would be cut down in a short time and with little effort from you!

Praying in the spirit is like using that power saw. Do you have to use it? No. Are you any less of a person for not using it? No. You don't have to use this amazing gift from God, but it sure gets the job done quicker and easier. Praying in tongues gets you and your small thinking (that hasn't been recreated) out of the equation. In other words, it leaves out the middleman to streamline your prayer.

Keep a journal with you during your prayer time as well. It is a good practice to write down anything you feel that the Lord is speaking to you. He will speak to you through His Word, but He will also speak directly to you – how exciting!

4. Be Thankful

Whatever you focus your attention on is what you will notice more of. Have you ever bought a car and thought you had the only one like it until you drove it off the lot and saw the same vehicle everywhere you looked? The truth is, those same cars were there all along, but what you think about is what you will see more of.

Being thankful is something that Christians and non-Christians alike recognize the benefits of. The key difference is that Christians direct their thanks to God, the Giver of all things. Ephesians 5:20 says, *"giving thanks always for all things to God the Father in the name of our Lord Jesus Christ."*

We have two instructions in Ephesians 5:20. The first is that we are to give thanks ALWAYS. Well, if you always have a thankful heart, it doesn't leave room for complaining and being negative. You have a choice as to what you want to see in any given situation. Will you notice the negative aspects or the positive ones? Being thankful isn't denying when your circumstances are bad, but even in the worse circumstances, you can thank God that He is with you and His Word promises that He will never leave your side.

The second instruction regarding giving of thanks is that you are to be thankful for all things. As I just said, you shouldn't be thankful for the bad circumstances in your life, but for God working on your behalf in the midst of that difficult circumstance. James 1:2-3 says, *"My brethren, count it all joy when you fall into various trials, knowing that the testing of your faith produces patience."* Just as lifting weights strengthens your body, going through trials will strengthen your faith if you keep focused on the answer – Jesus Christ. Remember that God does not cause the trial. The trial is a part of this life, but He will provide a way of escape from it.

Be conscious of being thankful for the little, seemingly mundane things in your life. For example, be thankful for a house to clean, for clothes to wash, for beds to be made, for meals to be cooked. Why? Because it means that you have shelter and warmth; you have a family to care for; you have money and food available to cook a meal.

Thankfulness is also a part of faith. It is thanking God for the promises He made in His Word for you before you have seen the manifestation of it. I thanked God for a strong marriage before I said, "I do." Before I had children, I thanked God for the children in my future. Before I was a pastor, I thanked God for wisdom and guidance to lead others. While I am healthy, I thank God for my health and that by His stripes, I was healed. (1 Pet. 2:24) Before I was debt-free, I thanked God for His provision and prosperity to live debt-free.

I am thankful that God is faithful and that what He promised us is true. I am thankful for my talents and abilities that He has placed in me to do what He has called me to do. If you haven't already done so, start a gratitude journal in which you record something that you are thankful for each day. Recognize that it is by His grace that you have what you have and can do what you can do.

5. Exercise

Whether you like it or not, your body needs exercise to function properly. We have all heard the benefits of exercise and how important it is to our bodies. Why is it that so many people refuse to do it then? I have heard many excuses (and have made them myself) from lack of time to physical limitations and everything in between. The truth of the matter is: You will find the time and the way to do something if you believe in the value of it.

I started exercising regularly around ten years ago. Before then, I would maybe exercise once in a while, but I definitely wasn't consistent. I had many excuses for not exercising, but the truth is, I just didn't want to do it. That all changed when my back started having a lot of problems and would go out quite frequently in my 20s and early 30s. I thought that I was much too young to have such terrible back problems. So, I started exercising and found that my back would start feeling better as long as I kept up with my exercises. I can testify that since I started consistently working out 2-6 times a week, my back hasn't gone out once in many years. Another wonderful side effect of exercise is that I am more productive during my day. I am more focused and energetic and get much more accomplished.

To remain consistent with my physical health, I had to make a switch in my thinking from "I HAVE to exercise" to "I GET to exercise." To be able to do physically what God has for me to do motivates me to be healthy. I want to have the energy to keep up with my kids and someday my grandkids. I want to travel. I want to eat a cookie or piece of cake here or there without feeling guilty about it.

Besides the physical benefits to exercise, I also have found that being active helps keep anxiety away – which is why I have included it in this chapter. I'm not a health expert, but I have experienced what the experts claim to be true about exercise. It helped to decrease drastically the stress and anxiety I experienced. If you are serious about getting rid of anxiety without being tied to medication, don't TRY to make exercise a part of your daily routine, schedule it in and do it!

Start simple –Try some of the following in your daily life:

- Do some simple stretches in the morning to wake up your body.
- Park your car further away from a store to allow more walking.
- Take the stairs instead of the elevator.
- Go for a walk during your lunch break.
- Have a dance party with your kids.
- Do some squats while brushing your teeth (I do this every night).

The most important thing is to change your mindset that exercise is bad. Remember that you are a steward of your body, which means that you are to take care of yourself.

One of the best resources I can give you for your health is faithfulworkouts.com. This site offers workouts for every level and time frame. There is a daily calendar, which provides options for beginners to those more advanced. The calendar also includes a healthy menu plan and a short devotion. Some of the videos are totally FREE. They have seriously gotten rid of any excuse you could come up with. I'm telling you, go right now and check it out!

I have been "faithful" to these workouts for many years. The reason I like this program so much is for all of the benefits listed above. The reason I keep going back is because they place the focus on being healthy, spirit, soul, and body. If you are not on your physical health journey with God, then back up and bring Him along. Having your spirit and soul connected to your workout will give that time more purpose and meaning. You will be getting healthy for God's glory, not your own. Let me also say that 'healthy' comes in all shapes and sizes. Again, as you seek Him, all of these things (including your health) will be added to you.

MAKE YOURSELF ACCOUNTABLE

When I was serious about creating and maintaining positive habits in my own life, I started making myself accountable to do them. I wrote each daily habit down in a way I could check them off when completed. Again, I find great satisfaction in checking items off of a list; therefore, this system really works for me.

In addition to keeping yourself accountable, give permission to a friend or even a pastor to come along beside you and help keep you accountable to your new goals and habits. You will do much better with a support system. Knowing that someone will be checking in on you will be beneficial.

The bottom line is that to maintain an anxiety-free life, you must be purposeful and consistent. You have to fight against self-sabotaging habits such as procrastination and making excuses. Just do what you know to do and leave the rest in God's hands.

HAVE A STRONG GAME PLAN

In order to win a sporting championship, you have to have a wise coach, strong offense, strong defense, and great teammates. When you play a sport, your opponent constantly changes. With that change, a coach and players will adjust their strategy to some degree, but they will never stray too far from the offensive and defensive plays they practice day in and day out. Executing the correct plays with the guidance of a wise coach will bring victory after victory.

Being coachable will win or lose games. It doesn't matter how talented a player is, if he/she is unwilling to listen to his/her coach, that player will not go very far. However, those who keep an ear to their coach and not only listen but obey the coach's instruction will find success.

The same is true for being a champion over your life. The Holy Spirit is your coach. The Bible refers to Him as your Helper. He has studied the 'game tape' of your opponents and knows how to win the game. He will show you where to make adjustments in your life so you are in position to get the victory.

My band teacher in high school had a saying that has stuck with me to this day. Mr. T. would say, "Practice doesn't make perfect. Perfect practice makes perfect." To be able to execute a play well, it has to be well-practiced. The success that we witness great athletes attain in a game is a result of hours and hours of discipline and practice. The most successful athletes are those who can be found on their own time, putting in the hard work and diligence to build and refine their innate abilities. They are not only putting in the practice time but approach their practice time strategically and diligently.

Having both a strong offense and defense is crucial to the winning recipe as well. If you apply what I have taught you in this book, I guarantee you will find success. Remember to never go against your opponent, the devil, without the Word. There are many different strategies that your Coach, the Holy Spirit, will give you, but you can never win in your own abilities. You must have the Word of God to back you up.

CHAPTER 10

REFLECTION QUESTIONS

1. What habits do you have that have helped you? What habits do you need to change?

2. What type of plan is needed for your life right now? Are you disciplined with your time? Why or why not?

3. If you haven't done so already, schedule your quiet time with God and purpose to meet with Him every day.

4. Begin a gratitude journal listing big, as well as seemingly insignificant things that you are thankful for each day. What are you thankful for today?

5. What are your feelings toward exercise? What can you start doing today (even if it's small) to start your journey to better physical health?

Closing

My prayer is that as you have read this book, you have found valuable insights and answers to handle anxiety and develop a peace-filled life. I hope you took advantage of the video lessons as well as the reflection prompts at the end of each chapter for a deeper, more personal journey. In conclusion, I want to review the important points from each chapter.

TRUST GOD

In order to release your worries, anxieties, and cares to God, you must have a relationship with Him. You must fully trust who He is and that He has great plans for you. The best way to build your trust in God is to spend time with Him in prayer and in the Word. You have to *plant* yourself in His care and allow Him access to your life.

REALIZE YOUR TRUE IDENTITY

Your true identity is who God says you are. This means that you must take off the labels you have been given by others or even yourself and accept who God says you are.

You must also have an understanding of how you were made. You are a spirit: You were made righteous the moment you asked Jesus into your heart and reserved your place in Heaven forever.

You have a soul: Your soul is comprised of your thoughts, will, and emotions. Your soul will also go to Heaven with your spirit; however, it has not been recreated. We must renew our minds constantly with the Word of God.

You live in a body: Your body enables you to live in this earth realm.

Just as an astronaut needs a spacesuit in space, you need a body (your earth suit) to operate on earth.

You are valuable to God and worthy to be loved and cared for by Him. Don't ever doubt His unconditional love for you. Unconditional means that He doesn't have certain conditions you have to meet to come to Him. He loves you without any strings attached.

GOD IS GOOD. THE DEVIL IS BAD

Plain and simple – there is a God and He is good. There is no evil in Him. On the other hand, there is also a devil, Satan, who is nothing but bad. There is no good in Him.

Use John 10:10 to determine if what you are going through or what you are facing is from God or from the devil. Remember that Jesus came to give you abundant life in every way. We are to lay hold of that abundant life by faith through love. When anxiety or any other fear comes knocking on your door, refuse to accept it.

HEALTHY SOUL = HEALTHY LIFE

Remember that when your mental health is good, your life will be good. 3 John 2 says, *"Beloved, I pray that you may prosper in all things and be in health, just as your soul prospers."* The battle you face day-in and day-out is in the realm of your mind. Spend time in the Word of God to strengthen and renew your soul and create a healthy life for yourself.

You don't have to be ruled by your feelings. You can make a conscious choice to smile even though your emotions are telling you to frown and sulk. This doesn't mean that you are denying your feelings, but rather, you are not going to let your feelings control you. Remember that your emotions are just a tool that can often be wrong.

Renew your mind with the Word of God. True change in your soul comes from getting in the Word and spending time with God. It doesn't take long in the presence of God to get a change of attitude and a new perspective. Unfortunately, mind renewal doesn't happen quickly. You have to be diligent and consistent in your time with God.

ACTIVATE FAITH OR FEAR BY YOUR WORDS

Because you were created in the image of God, you also are to operate as He does. God designed our words to actually have creative power. You can create the life you want for yourself through your words.

When we speak God's Word in faith, it brings those promises of an abundant life into reality. On the other hand, when you speak worry all the time, you are actually speaking those worries into reality.

Instead of proclaiming yourself as a professional worrier, start declaring that you are a professional believer! You take what God says in the Bible as truth and believe every Word. Adopt the motto, "If God said it, I believe it and that settles it!"

THERE IS NO TIME LIKE THE PRESENT

Living in faith instead of fear and anxiety comes down to living in the now. Wrongs done to you will hold you in bondage to the past, and fear of the future will keep you from moving forward or making right choices.

The most powerful resource you have is your time. Budgeting your time is just as important as budgeting your money. When you purpose to seek God first with your time (and your finances), everything else will fall into place. Matthew 6:33 says that everything that you are worrying about and fretting over will be taken care of when you seek God first.

Be grateful for everything in your life - big and small. A grateful heart causes you to have a positive outlook on everything around you. You have a choice to see your world from a "glass half full or half empty" mindset. Choose to create an attitude of gratitude in all you do.

CAST ALL OF YOUR CARE ON GOD

Casting your care on God boils down to this: When you work, God rests; when you rest, God works. God is a gentleman who isn't going to overstep His welcome. He can only take care of what you give Him to take care of. As long as you are dealing with your problems yourself, He will not take over. However, as soon as you are ready to give Him ALL of your care, He will go to work for you, making the crooked places straight in your life (Isaiah 45: 2). You were never meant to handle the problems of this life in and by yourself. Casting your care on God enables God to work on your behalf.

Taking back your care is like telling your children to do a certain chore and then taking over when they don't do it the way you want it done. Control is a hard thing to give up, but when you give God access to your problems by casting them on Him, your situation will miraculously change for the better.

WATCH OUT

There are many ways that the devil snares us into a life of fear and anxiety. It would be nice if there was a red flag on everything the devil is using, but that isn't the case. There might not be a red flag that you can see; however, the Holy Spirit will light a red flag in your spirit if you are paying attention to Him. The problem is that the longer we live like the world (non-Christians) and act like the world, it will be harder to identify what the devil is using. Many times, we have adopted ways of thinking and acting from friends, family, and our surroundings that have become comfortable. We may not think anything of what we watch, listen to, read, or whom we have relationships with. Remember that God's ways are higher than your ways, and His thoughts are higher than your thoughts.

PLANT AND GROW

When I forget to water my houseplants (which I often do), they become shriveled and start dying. They need water to survive and so do you. Yes, you need actual water, but you also need spiritual water found in Christ. The place of peace, security, and abundance is found in Jesus. Plant yourself by the rivers of living water by reading your Bible, listening to good teaching, and spending time in prayer.

Let unforgiveness and bitterness fall away and follow the commandment of love. Believe God's promises and receive them by faith. This is how to stay in a place of peace and security. This doesn't mean that bad things will never happen to you ever again. It just means that you are equipped and ready to take on anything the devil throws at you. When the devil looks for you, let him find you hiding in Jesus, the one who already defeated him for good.

CREATE GREAT HABITS

This new life doesn't just happen. We are humans who default to the habits we have created for ourselves. The good news is that we can actually re-wire our default system and build new healthy habits. You can build yourself supports for living an anxiety-free life.

Building new habits takes will power and diligence. However, as you may have noticed, your will power is like a battery that doesn't have a very long and sustaining life. As you are diligent to use your will power to build one or two habits at a time, the habits take over allowing you to use your will power on another task. I suggest beginning with the most important and essential habits - Bible time and prayer time. You cannot expect a positive change in your life without being connected to your Maker.

FINAL THOUGHTS

My prayer is that after reading this book and taking advantage of the reflection questions in each chapter, you experience a positive change in your life.

Anxiety is a strange phenomenon. It attacks your mind and body, taking full control of your being. Anxiety will always try to get you to crumble under its pressure. Even though you can be doing all the right things and staying connected to God, anxiety will still try to knock on your door. Knowing how to handle it when it does come is vital.

I have mentioned Dr. Caroline Leaf before, and I again strongly suggest her material. I recently read a blog post from her about how to handle anxiety she said, "Anxiety provides the opportunity for change because it signals what is wrong and what is causing damage in our brains and bodies—it tells us what needs to be addressed in our lives. Life is, of course, a process, an ongoing series of events, many of which are challenging, and anxiety can actually be one of our greatest teachers."

I have learned that when anxiety strikes to examine myself. I take a moment to think about what I was thinking about or what caused the anxiety to surface. When you can logically look at the source of your anxiety, it allows you to give that anxiety-filled thought to God. You can cast that care on Him because He cares for you. When you fully give it to God, He will transform that anxiety into peace.

Plant yourself in God's goodness.
Plant yourself in God's grace.
See yourself as the victor,
at the end of your life's race.
Plant yourself in the Word of God,
Attend to it each day.
Put it down into your heart,
so you will know just what to say.
Plant yourself in the here and now,
Don't worry about the future or the past.
Plant yourself in His mighty love,
Forgiving your hurts at last.
Plant yourself in faith,
Refuse to fear or be afraid.
Cast your care on God,
Make the greatest trade.
Plant yourself in prayer,
Listen to the Holy Ghost.
Plant yourself in the Prince of Peace,
He's the one you need the most.
Plant yourself by the Rivers of Water,
the place where abundant life flows.
Plant yourself, refuse to move
And watch how you blossom and grow.

References

Facts and Statistics. (2018). Retrieved September, 2018, from https://adda. org/about-adda/press-room/facts-statistics

Helgeland, B. (Director). (2001). A Knight's Tale [Video file]. United States: Columbia Pictures.

Leaf, Caroline. (2019). Retrieved 2018, from https://drleaf.com/

Oz, F. (Director), Ziskin, L. (Producer), & Schulman, T. (Writer). (1991). What about Bob? [Motion picture]. United States: Buena Vista Pictures Distribution, Inc.

Savelle Foy, T. (2018). 5 Things Successful People Do Before 8 am. Rockwall, TX: Terri Savelle Foy Ministries.

Spadafora, M. (Faithful Workouts. Retrieved September 2018, From https://www.faithfulworkouts.com/

Prayer for Salvation and Baptism in the Holy Spirit

Heavenly Father, I come to You in the Name of Jesus. Your Word says, "Whoever calls on the name of the Lord shall be saved" (Acts 2:21). I am calling on You. I pray and ask Jesus to come into my heart and be Lord over my life according to Romans 10:9-10: "If you confess with your mouth the Lord Jesus and believe in your heart that God has raised Him from the dead, you will be saved. For with the heart, one believes unto righteousness, and with the mouth, confession is made unto salvation." I do that now. I confess that Jesus is Lord, and I believe in my heart that God raised Him from the dead. I repent of sin. I renounce it. I renounce the devil and everything he stands for. Jesus is my Lord.

I am now reborn! I am a Christian – a child of Almighty God! I am saved! You also said in Your Word, "If you then, being evil, know how to give good gifts to your children, how much more will your Heavenly Father give the Holy Spirit to those who ask Him?" (Luke 11:13). I'm also asking You to fill me with the Holy Spirit. Holy Spirit, rise up within me as I praise God. I fully expect to speak with other tongues as You give me the utterance (Acts 2:4). In Jesus' Name. Amen!

About the Author

Colette Schaffer is known for her down to earth, straight-talking style of preaching and teaching the Word. She started her ministry with music in 2001; writing, recording and producing her first CD entitled, *Receive In Faith.* Colette is also the author of *Expecting Jesus: An Advent Devotional.*

Colette has been a pastor and teacher of the Word of God since 2006 after graduating from Rhema Bible College in Tulsa, OK. She and her husband are considered home missionaries as they currently pastor New Hope Church, located in Timber Lake, SD, on the Cheyenne River Reservation.

Colette has a passion for teaching how to live a peace-filled life. She has enjoyed hosting women's conferences through the years as her message centers around the foundations of faith and who we are in Christ, spirit, soul, and body. Colette emphasizes the importance of renewing one's mind with the Word of God. Colette also shares weekly insights on her blog at schafferministries.com.

Colette and her husband, Bryce Schaffer, have been married since 1995. They have three outstanding children: Ethan, Callie, and Nathanial.

Recommended Reading and Helpful Sources

Books

1. *5 Things Successful People Do Before 8 AM* by Terri Savelle Foy
2. *Who Switched Off My Brain* by Caroline Leaf
3. *To Know Him* by Gloria Copeland
4. *How to Stop Worrying and Start Living* by Dale Carnegie
5. *Hearing From Heaven* by Gloria Copeland
6. *Your 10-Day Spiritual Action Plan for Overcoming Stress, Anxiety and Depression* by Kenneth and Gloria Copeland
7. *"I forgive you, but…" 3 Steps that Can Heal Your Heart Forever* by Karen Jensen Salisbury

Websites

1. schafferministries.com
2. faithfulworkouts.com
3. kcm.org
4. karenjensen.org
5. drleaf.com

CPSIA information can be obtained
at www.ICGtesting.com
Printed in the USA
LVHW030924040420
652211LV00004B/1292